THE SOCIAL WORKERS

The
social
workers

EDITED BY
ALAN HANCOCK
AND
PHYLLIS WILLMOTT

BRITISH BROADCASTING CORPORATION

Published by the British Broadcasting Corporation
35 Marylebone High Street, London W.1

© British Broadcasting Corporation 1965
First published 1965

Printed in England by The Garden City Press Ltd
Letchworth Herts
No. 6271

CONTENTS

Preface

This collection of essays on social work and welfare arises directly from an educational television series for BBC-2. Under the general title of *The Social Workers* and transmitted during the Autumn and Winter of 1965 it gives an introductory survey of social work, in all the fields described in this book. Much of the series is on film and shows the social worker in action, in a variety of locations and under different conditions. Some of the contributors to this book have also helped with the television programmes, some are appearing in the broadcasts. But they all have a long and intimate association with different aspects of social work.

We have asked them, in these essays, to survey their own particular field, and indicate its special problems and special ways of overcoming them, describing in particular new and experimental approaches. Social work has developed considerably over recent years. It has become a vast complex of voluntary and statutory provision, involving both professional and voluntary workers. Techniques, methods and emphases are changing rapidly. More and more professional social workers are moving away from narrow specialisms, seeing themselves as partners in a general field. Problems of the individual, once treated in isolation are now viewed increasingly in the context of the family unit. We are moreover, beginning to look wider than the family circle, to the community at large, and to emphasise preventive work as much as the solution of immediate problems. The number of social workers is increasing, as more Younghusband and parallel courses get off the ground. But the demand for trained and voluntary workers also increases, as we begin to look at causes as much as at specific problems.

These essays are intended for readers who would like to go beyond the scope of the television broadcasts. For reasons of space, there are inevitable omissions, but taken together, they add up to an interim report on a developing field, a field which will become increasingly important over the next decade.

ALAN HANCOCK
and PHYLLIS WILLMOTT

The coming of social work

M. PENELOPE HALL

In this first essay Penelope Hall outlines the historical background of social work and the social worker. Miss Hall, now Senior Lecturer in the Department of Social Science at Liverpool University, has had earlier experience in social work and administration, especially in connection with councils of social service and associated voluntary organizations. She is author of *The social services of modern England* (6th edn. 1963) and, together with Ismene V. Howes, *The Church in social work* (1965).

At all times and in all places individuals and groups have given some kind of social care to one another in their need. This help may be given by one person to another without thought of return, and so contain within it the seeds of philanthropy. The roles of giver and receiver may be reversed, this is the basis of mutual aid.

Social care of this informal personal kind persists even in our complex modern societies, and the current emphasis in British social policy on what is known as 'community care' (the care of aged, handicapped and other dependent persons in their own homes and neighbourhoods) recognizes this.

But important as it is, it is now only one way of meeting need. As units of living have become larger, economic and social relationships more complex and the political situation more stable and highly organized, so the care of the poor and unfortunate has become increasingly widely recognized as a responsibility not only of their relatives and neighbours, but of the community as a whole. The process in this country had its beginnings in the middle ages, developed more rapidly from the Tudor period onward and can be traced in three main areas of private benevolence or philanthropy, mutual aid, and lastly, and most important and far reaching in its results, the gradual assumption by the political community or state for the welfare of its individual citizens.

Beginnings

In a recently published book Professor David Owen of Harvard University suggests that even before the beginning of the seventeenth century 'English charity had already taken on the dignity of a national tradition', and 'to give or leave something to the community – a fund for the poor, an almshouse, a grammar school – came to be expected of the more prosperous Englishman'.[1] During the closing years of this century, however, a new and far-reaching development which was to affect the whole character of charitable effort began to take place. This was the growth of collective effort by means of charitable organizations. Although individual effort continued, 'in the future the hallmark of the philanthropist was to be not merely generous giving, but also his support of worthy organizations'.[2] The growth of charitable institutions, many of them created through the group effort which was a noticeable characteristic of the eighteenth century, demonstrated the value and effectiveness of this collective action. For example, by means of the alliance between this new form of private philanthropy and the advancement of medical care hospitals were founded in all parts of the country – while a 'hospital' of another kind, the Foundling Hospital for the rescue, care and training of abandoned and deserted young infants proved the prototype of a network of charitable institutions dealing with social problems. These ranged from the 'reception, maintenance and employment of penitent prostitutes', the aim of the Magdalen Hospital, to the apprenticeship of poor boys to the sea, that of the

[1] David Owen *English philanthropy 1660–1960* Harvard U.P.; O.U.P., 1965, p. 2.   [2] *Ibid.*, p. 11.

8

Marine Society. The eighteenth century was, thus, an age of increasing private benevolence on the part of the wealthy mercantile class in particular. This was, according to Professor Owen, the product of a combination of Puritan piety, a benevolently humanitarian outlook and a concern for the national interest.[1]

In many fields the need for this kind of help was urgent and obvious; for example, Captain Coram was stirred to action by seeing abandoned young babies lying in the streets and on the dunghills of London. Moreover, at that time and for many generations to come there was no public provision outside the Poor Law which dated back to 1601. It is true that the scope of poor relief was wide, embracing all kinds of destitution, but outdoor relief was minimal and the institutional care given in the mixed workhouses of the period was at its best uninviting, at its worst intolerable to all but the most degraded. The Poor Law Amendment Act, 1834 made a considerable difference to the efficiency of the administration of poor relief, but the doctrinaire individualism and emphasis on the virtue of self-help meant that those who valued their self-respect applied for assistance only with the greatest reluctance.

Public provision in the first half of the nineteenth century being designedly repellent, and mutual aid still in its infancy, private charity continued to dominate the scene. Much of it was associated with the religious revivals, which were a feature of this period. Evangelicals were active in all forms of charitable effort associated with the relief of distress, but a characteristic of their work, which has particular relevance for the later development of social work, was the emphasis they placed on district visiting in which social care and assistance were combined with evangelization. Typical of these Missions was the London Bible and Domestic Mission founded in 1857 by a certain Mrs Ranyard. Dr Heasman in her book

[1] David Owen, *op. cit.*, p. 15.

The social workers

Evangelicals in action suggests that Mrs Ranyard's 'biblewomen' who carried out such work under the control of a lady superintendent were, in effect, the first paid social workers.[1] At about the same time the Female Mission to the Fallen was employing 'street missionaries', also under the guidance of a lady supervisor, to go out into the street at nights with the object of seeking out 'those (women) who are desirous of abandoning their evil ways'[2] and directing them to places of shelter. At about the same time (1862) the Ladies' Section of the Manchester and Salford Sanitary Association started to employ working class women to visit the poor in their own homes and instruct them in health and child care.

These 'homely women' were the forerunners of the present day health visitors. Most professional social workers trace their direct line of descent through a tradition of much more organized 'scientific' charity which culminated in the founding of the London Charity Organization Society in 1869.

Charity Organization Society

The Charity Organization Society was conceived as an attempt to co-ordinate the work of charities and charitable organizations with one another and with the Poor Law. 'It failed, as it was perhaps bound to do' but it has left us a legacy of enduring value, for in carrying out its idea of charity the Charity Organization Society used and popularized the method of casework and helped to found the profession of social workers.[3] It was not that the principles and precepts on which the Society based its social work was new. A Scottish minister, Thomas

[1] Kathleen Heasman *Evangelicals in action: an appraisal of their social work in the Victorian era* Bles, 1962, p. 37.

[2] M. Penelope Hall and Ismene V. Howes *The Church in social work: a study of moral welfare work undertaken by the Church of England* Routledge, 1965, p. 26.

[3] C. L. Mowat *The Charity Organisation Society, 1869–1913* Methuen, 1961, p. 2.

Chalmers, was expounding and preaching somewhat similar ones in his Glasgow parish in the early years of the century, and certain charitable organizations founded in its middle years carried on his tradition. But 'it remained for the Charity Organization Society to codify these techniques, to transmit them from one worker to another, and, in doing so, to lay the foundation for a profession of social work with its own discipline and its own ethics'.[1]

The type of social work which the Charity Organization Society and those associated with it, such as Octavia Hill, were endeavouring to practice sought to be both individual in its concern and scientific in its approach. As Una Cormack writes about Octavia Hill, 'Her contribution to the theory of case-work was her long experience that power to help anyone depended upon knowledge and friendship'.[2] The work was focused not so much on the problem of poverty, the existence of which appeared to be accepted as part of the natural order, but on the moral degradation which accompanied it. This 'pauperism' could only be overcome by means of planned constructive help to individuals and families, starting with careful investigation, including, at least in all deserving cases, 'judicious and effectual assistance'[3] and aiming at restoration of self-respect and independence.

This type of support and assistance, time consuming as it was, was carried out during the Society's early years by an army of voluntary workers, assisted from the earliest days by paid Inquiry Agents. These were often men of working class origin, and whose status was com-

---

[1] K. Woodroofe, *From charity to social work in England and the United States*. Routledge, 1962, p. 24.

[2] Una Cormack 'Developments in case-work', chapter 3 of A. F. C. Bourdillon *Voluntary social services: their place in the modern state* (Nuffield College Social Reconstruction Survey) Methuen, 1945, p. 97.

[3] Taken from a statement of principles which appeared in the Society's annual report for 1875 and is quoted in C. L. Mowat, *op cit.*, pp. 25–6.

paratively lowly and salary small. As time went on, however, and as the work extended and standards became more rigorous, district secretaries, 'paid officers of good education, character and address' began to be appointed, not only to undertake casework but to organize the work in their area and train volunteers. Training had come to be regarded as essential and by 1896 the Society had combined with the Women's University Settlement in Southwark and the National Union of Women Workers to organize lectures in addition to the supervized practical experience which was the basis of such training.[1]

Of all Victorian charitable institutions for the relief of distress, the Charity Organization Society, with offshoots in the provinces and in America, had the most widespread and lasting influence on the development of social casework. The social settlements, founded in East London also during the latter years of the nineteenth century, probably contributed most to group and neighbourhood work. They were not alone in their endeavours, since they had been preceded in youth work alone by such organizations as the Y.M.C.A. and Y.W.C.A. dating back to the eighteen forties and fifties, and by the assortment of clubs and associations which followed them. The aim of bringing the highly educated and greatly privileged not only to work but to live among the poor and underprivileged as their friends and neighbours, was a new departure. 'I came to the conclusion that such places represent simply a protest against the sin of taking things for granted, in particular taking one's own social position or conditions for granted', wrote one of the most distinguished of the second generation of settlers, William Beveridge, in 1904.[2]

The settlements were, at their best, a real attempt to

[1] C. L. Mowat, *op. cit.*, p. 102–4.
[2] Lord Beveridge *Power and influence* Hodder & Stoughton, 1953, p. 30.

understand the problems of the poor by sharing in them, despite a certain artificiality and perhaps even patronage.[1] The realization grew that problems were not only associated with individual misfortune and personal inadequacy but were also collective, deriving from economic and social causes. Not only did settlements undertake such projects for individual well-being as Poor Man's Lawyer services, together with clubs and other group projects, they also sponsored investigations into social conditions and led campaigns for social improvement. 'There is indeed scarcely any field of social legislation or any statutory instrument of social service which does not owe something of its inception or direction to the recorded observations or voluntary experiments of settlers who, year by year, followed the call of Samuel Barnett (the founder of the first settlement, Toynbee Hall, Whitechapel) to those mean streets where their fellow citizens led anxious, meagre lives', contends the historian of the Manchester University Settlement.[2]

Reforms

In general nineteenth century philanthropists stood a little apart from those who were pressing for statutory responsibility in public welfare.

During the early years of the nineteenth century *laissez-faire* individualism combined with Malthusian theories of population growth to restrict government intervention in economic and social affairs within very narrow limits. However the health and social problems associated with the rapid increase of the population and its concentration in towns; the manifest evils of child

[1] K. Woodroofe, *op. cit.*, quotes a later observer, 'obviously soured by his experience of American settlements', who suggested that 'the residents seemed bent on reaching down to help the poor climb not quite up to the level of their benefactors'.

[2] Mary Stocks *Fifty years in Every Street: the story of the Manchester University settlement* Manchester U.P., 1945, p. 5.

labour in factories and mines; the educational challenge of an age in which scientific and technical advance were the prerequisites of national prosperity; the growing power of the working classes, all these combined as the century went on to modify attitudes towards more widespread and varied public provision. The two most important areas in which these developments took place were undoubtedly public health and elementary education, though there were others, for example, public parks and libraries. It was not only community provision that was required; equally important was restrictive action through legislation. Thus the first measures to be taken in connection with housing were the imposition of minimum standards on private house builders and the clearance of slums, and the public provision of houses to accommodate the slum dwellers followed on from this.[1] By the end of the century the necessity of community provision for the protection of the individual from such hazards as disease and the worst evils of economic exploitation had been accepted, and so had the elementary education of the poor at public expense. But although there had been some preliminary skirmishes, the battle had not yet been joined over the question of public responsibility for ensuring minimum standards of personal well-being. The main issue was that of income maintenance: this involved overcoming preconceived ideas and facing the problem of poverty as distinct from that of pauperism.

The supporters of the Charity Organization Society assumed that the causes of distress were personal, to be overcome by patient understanding casework directed towards individuals and families. They did not accept any inherent defects in the economic and social system,

[1] For an account of these developments see William Ashworth *The genesis of modern British town planning: a study in economic and social history of the nineteenth and twentieth centuries* Routledge, 1954.

14

and in doing so they were thinking and acting in accordance with the dominant orthodoxy of their time. During the last thirty years of the nineteenth century, however, this orthodoxy received a number of shocks which in the end engendered a new attitude to social problems. The depression of the 1880s with its concomitant mass unemployment brought home to the public the fact that 'the unemployed were not necessarily or even mainly weaklings or idlers, but the product of an impersonal phenomenon called "unemployment", a word that had only recently been introduced into the vocabulary'. A few years later the strikes of the match-girls and the dockers voiced the complaints of 'men and women whose labour was in demand, but who were not thereby enabled to rescue themselves from conditions of extreme poverty'.[1] Meanwhile, Charles Booth, a Liverpool ship-owner, was devoting his time, talents and fortune to a major scientific investigation *The life and labour of the people in London*. This originated as an attempt to discover the extent and causes of what Booth himself regarded as 'the problem of all problems', the problem of poverty.[2]

Booth's survey, and its successors (notably B. Seebohm Rowntree's detailed study of York published in 1901[3]) were, whatever their methodological limitations, objective and factual assessments of the current situation and could not be ignored.

They revealed that not only was poverty, measured in terms of a bare sufficiency of the means of livelihood, widespread, but it was to be found not solely among the thriftless, drunken and idle, but among the respectable

[1] T. H. Marshall *Social policy* Hutchinson, 1965. p. 23.

[2] For an assessment of Booth's contribution to social policy and social science see T. S. & M. Simey *Charles Booth: social scientist* O.U.P., 1960.

[3] B. Seebohm Rowntree *Poverty: a study of town life* Macmillan, 1901.

15

and hard-working. Those, if they were badly paid unskilled labourers, had a large family of young children, or were unemployed, sick or old, might well find themselves living below the poverty line. 'Of all the causes of primary poverty which have been brought to our notice,' wrote another investigator, Professor A. L. Bowlby, 'low wages are by far the most important.' Other tasks revealed by these and related investigations, such as the Report of the Interdepartmental Committee on Physical Deterioration published in 1904, were to feed necessitous schoolchildren and keep a check on physical development; to introduce some scheme of income maintenance in old age which would not be associated in any way with the hated Poor Law; to provide minimum wage legislation in connection with what were known as the 'sweated industries', and some kind of sickness and unemployment benefit.

These tasks were tackled with vigour and enthusiasm by the Liberal government elected in 1906 and the years which followed were among the formative years of what was later to be called the 'welfare state'. Unfortunately, however, this period of rapid development in social provision coincided with a period of relative stagnation in social work, a time, moreover, when the long-standing opposition of the Charity Organization Society to any form of state intervention hardened under attack, so that its supporters and associates were regarded by the reformers as rigid and obscurantist in their outlook and practice. As a result professional social workers played 'almost no part' in these 'immense advances in social betterment and their ideas and experience were not incorporated into the main stream of social policy until the time of the Second World War.'[1]

Until the Second World War, the majority of social workers stood a little aside from the developments in

[1] Eileen Younghusband *Social work and social change* Allen and Unwin, 1964, p. 18.

social policy and social legislation taking place around them. But they were, during this period, consolidating their position in certain administrative settings and establishing themselves in others. Almoners, to give them their traditional title, only recently abandoned, were already established in voluntary hospitals in London by the turn of the century and medical social work, as it is now called, has become one of the most widely recognized of the social work professions. A few years later, in 1907, the Probation of Offenders Act not only accepted the principle of supervising offenders as an alternative to imprisonment but provided for the statutory appointment of probation officers and their payment from public funds. This provision was, in effect, a recognition of work already being undertaken under religious auspices by the police court missionaries, but it was nevertheless the first step towards an official service of social workers attached to the courts, and indeed of any official 'casework' service in this country at all.[1] Meanwhile larger and more progressive firms were already appointing welfare workers to be responsible for the general well-being of their employees, a development accelerated during the First World War.

A significant characteristic of these developments in professional social work was that they involved specialization, and in this country until comparatively recently social work has been practised by a group of separate, even if related, professions, each working in its own administrative setting. The emphasis has thus been on diversity rather than unity though this situation is now changing. During the inter-war period a new specialization was introduced when psychiatric social workers, the earliest of whom were trained in the U.S.A., began to practise alongside psychiatrists in both mental hospitals and the newly created child guidance clinics.

[1] Joan S. King (ed.) *The probation service* Butterworth, first edition, 1958, p. 9.

The social workers

These carefully selected and highly trained specialists were very influential in setting the tone and determining the future pattern of social work. In particular they acted as intermediaries in the passage to this country of the new approach to social casework which was currently sweeping the U.S.A. This approach stressed the close association between social casework and psychotherapy and was preoccupied with psychological rather than economic needs and problems. Although in the long run the impact of this new approach was considerable, at first it was not very noticeable. The most serious social problems of the inter-war period, and the ones which received most attention, were those associated with prolonged unemployment and, aside from the policy issues connected with income maintenance, energies were concentrated on such schemes for maintaining the morale of the unemployed as the provision of allotments and the promotion of clubs. The emphasis was on group and community work embodying a large element of self-help and mutual aid. The same emphasis was to be found in the community developments taking place on the vast new housing estates.

The Second World War and after

The effects of the Second World War on the future pattern of social policy and administration, and hence on the role and status of the social worker, were profound and far reaching.[1] In the first place the war imposed a very considerable strain, sometimes an unbearable strain, on the many families whose way of life was disturbed and changed by evacuation, dispersal through bombing and the mobilization of man and woman power. Moreover, these disturbances sometimes affected not only

[1] They are discussed in detail in R. M. Titmuss *Problems of social policy* 1950, and its companion volume, S. Ferguson and H. Fitzgerald *Studies in the social services* 1954. (History of the Second World War, United Kingdom civil series) H.M.S.O. and Longmans.

individual families but whole neighbourhoods. This meant that families were increasingly unable to deal unaided with normal contingencies of life such as birth or sickness, while in addition they were faced with the abnormal contingencies brought about by the war. 'What the family and neighbourhood could no longer do for themselves the State had to help them to do. The social services, therefore, far from being reduced in wartime had to be expanded.'[1]

Nor was it only family needs that led to the expansion of the social services. As their problems came to the fore it was recognized that there were special groups whose needs had been accentuated by the war, and for whom special provision should be made. Thus, during the autumn of 1939 the Board of Education (as it then was) found time, even in the midst of the educational dislocation caused by the evacuation, to formulate plans for a 'Service of Youth', in which local education authorities and voluntary organizations would unite to meet the social and recreational needs of young people. Rather later, by which time the problem had assumed sizeable proportions, the Ministry of Health issued a circular[2] urging local welfare authorities to prepare schemes making special provision for the social care of unmarried mothers and their children. Other examples of social services envisaged and provided to meet special needs as the war went on were day nurseries intended specifically to help solve the problems of the married woman worker, residential nurseries, and hostels for maladjusted children and for old people.

In its efforts to find ways of meeting the social needs of wartime the government made full use of both the local authorities and the voluntary organizations. These organizations were, in the main, ready and willing to co-operate, and in the circumstances adjusted themselves

---

[1] S. M. Ferguson and H. Fitzgerald, *op. cit.*, p. 7.
[2] Ministry of Health, Circular 2866, October 1943.

willingly to what proved to be a changing pattern of relationships with the State. Inevitably war meant increased central government control and more comprehensive planning, and of necessity voluntary agencies had to adjust their own plans so that they fitted into this pattern. But within these limits many organizations showed considerable enterprise and initiative and made their own special contributions to meeting particular needs. One such contribution which was later incorporated into the pattern of the post-war social services was the Citizens' Advice Bureaux service. This was established in several areas to deal with the many requests for advice and information which the changes and dislocations of war would inevitably bring.

Another arose from the efforts of a small group of pacifists to further, by means of patient, persistent friendship and help, the social rehabilitation of a number of bombed out families whose standards and manner of life were causing serious concern to the officials. Enlarged, and professionalized these efforts have been transformed into the intensive casework service now rendered to families with multiple problems by Family Service Units.

The work undertaken by Pacifist Service Units, as they were then known, was a particular type of intensive social care, and during the war it soon became evident that wartime conditions were increasing the need for social care as well as for social provision. This meant that 'war conditions made new demands upon social workers and gave them unprecedented opportunities'.[1] At first the nature and value of their skills was hardly appreciated by the authorities, but by the middle years of the war this attitude was changing, and social workers began to be employed by regional and local authorities, for example, in connection with evacuation schemes.[2] By the end of the

[1] U. Cormack, *op. cit.*, p. 109.
[2] R. M. Titmuss, *op. cit.*, p. 381.

war they had achieved higher status and greater recognition than they were accorded at the beginning.

Far more important than any of the wartime developments discussed so far was, however, the new attitude towards statutory social service provision engendered by the shared experiences of wartime. Not only were there risks, to which all were liable (though not equally so) there were also shortages and hardships, and it was generally accepted that these should also be shared. The relative success of such wartime measures as food and clothes rationing was a measure of this acceptance and the strong feeling of national solidarity.

In this situation 'it was increasingly regarded as a proper function and even obligation of government to ward off stress and strain among not only the poor but almost all classes of society'. The wartime social services, like the wartime controls, were intended to be comprehensive in scope, if not as yet universal in character. 'By the end of the Second World War the government had, through the agency of newly established and existing services, assumed and developed a measure of direct concern for the health and well-being of the population which, by contrast with the role of government in the nineteen thirties was little short of remarkable'.[1]

What was perhaps equally remarkable was the way in which during the war plans were made to carry over into the post-war era the wartime assumption that 'social policy consisted of services rendered by the society as a whole to the society as a whole'.[2] In concrete terms this change of outlook involved the planning of a comprehensive scheme of social security out of the existing confused inadequate and disparate arrangements, a task undertaken by William Beveridge and his committee of advisers. Other reforms planned at this time were: a

[1] R. M. Titmuss, *op. cit.*, p. 506.
[2] T. H. Marshall, *op. cit.*, p. 88.

21

comprehensive National Health Service, the reform of the educational system to provide 'secondary education for all'; other problems such as the major issues of housing and town planning were also tackled, and important reforms in connection with the care of the deprived child. In all this the emphasis was on social provision available to the user as of right. It was assumed that people making use of the services were, in general, responsible, capable of running their own affairs, and differing from their fellows only in their lack of something which the community could and should provide. It could be argued and was argued that in this setting the task of the social worker is 'to individualize social services and institutions in order to direct clients' attention to the forms of practical assistance relevant to their problems'.[1]

The widening of statutory responsibility to ensure at least a 'minimum standard of civilized living'[2] for all citizens was perhaps the major achievement of the immediate post-war social legislation. But a rather different approach is inherent in some at least of the legislation of the period (for example the National Assistance and Children Act) and has been developed since. This is epitomized in the constant use of the term 'welfare'. This term, particularly when used in such phrases as 'the welfare of the child' or 'the welfare of the persons assisted', implies that social care should be suited to the needs and circumstances of the individual. This brings the social worker into the very centre of social service provision. A noticeable contrast between the pre-war situation and the present is that the professional social worker was more likely to be working in a voluntary rather than in a statutory setting, but now it is the

---

[1] K. Woodroofe, *op. cit.*, p. 147, cf. Barbara Wootton *Social science and social pathology* Allen & Unwin, 1959, Ch. IX.

[2] Beatrice Webb *Our partnership* Longmans, 1948, p. 482.

statutory services, particularly the child care services which are absorbing new recruits to the profession and crying out for more. Furthermore, whereas before the war it was widely assumed that a statutory agency was too rigid and impersonal to provide a satisfactory setting for the handling of intricate and delicate problems, this proposition, always of doubtful validity, can no longer be maintained. We have only to look at the intricacy of the problems handled by, for example, psychiatric social workers in the mental health services, child care officers and probation officers.

The present day

One of the issues frequently raised in connection with the expansion of the social services, particularly the statutory social services, is that of the spheres of public and family responsibility. Much of present day social provision is made in respect of dependent groups such as children or elderly persons who traditionally have been expected to rely on their own families for support. Consequently the social services have been frequently indicted on the score that they weaken family responsibility. In this connection, however, a distinction should be made between providing a service which is a substitute for some form of care which otherwise might be provided by the family, and a service which supplements the care given by the family and enables it to discharge its responsibilities more efficiently and with less strain. The tendency of recent years has been to stress the latter kind of service rather than the former.

Wherever the emphases in social provision are placed there are certain prerequisites for its success. In the first place it demands at least a reasonably satisfactory physical environment. We have done much to overcome most evils of gross poverty and widespread squalor but there are still areas and situations in which life is being lived below the minimum. London's homeless are an example of this.[1]

A second prerequisite is co-operation. In this country the social services have grown up as specialist services providing for special needs and the social work professions as specialist professions. It is now realized that this approach, important as it was in order to establish the claims of the individual, consideration is inadequate in that it gives insufficient attention to the role of both family and community. The training of social workers is now becoming more 'generic' in character. There are signs that group and community work whose development has lagged behind that of case work are at last coming into their own.[2] There are also signs that several existing specialist services may, in the long run, be integrated as some form of local authority family service. But in most areas this is likely to be a long term process and meanwhile there are various means of co-operation and co-ordination which can be utilized with advantage to all concerned.

Co-operation does not simply mean co-operation among social workers and administrators engaged in helping people in need, however. It involves the participation of the person in need, his family and community. One of the interesting features of the present situation in social work and administration is the breaking down of the traditional distinction between casework, group work and community organization. Groups may be 'therapeutic', or a caseworker, such as a probation officer, find himself engaged in community activities in the interests of the prevention of delinquency. Meanwhile the multiplication of 'mutual aid' associations

[1] This problem is investigated and discussed in John Greve *London's homeless.* (Occasional papers on social administration, No. 10). Welwyn: Codicote P., 1964.

[2] M. Broady *Community power and voluntary initiative* in *Social Service Quarterly*, Winter 1964, pp. 89 ff.

among those suffering from a common misfortune, such as a physical handicap, and their propensity to act as pressure groups as well as means of mutual support is indicative of yet another development which adds to the variety of the present situation. This situation will be described in more detail and dicussed further in the following chapter.

Social work today

FLORENCE MITCHELL

In this essay Florence Mitchell gives a general survey of the scope, methods and problems of social work today.

Miss Mitchell trained for social work at University College, London, and the London School of Economics, taking a B.Sc.Econ. in Sociology. She has since worked for a local authority and for the Family Welfare Association, and is now Lecturer to the Two Year Social Work Course at Croydon Technical College. She recently assisted with the preparation of *Introduction to a social worker* (1964) for the National Institute for Social Work Training.

Social work, to most people not actively engaged in it, presents a blurred picture. For some it is still the benevolent ladies with baskets of goodies; for others it is the all-providing welfare state. Reactions to being told that one is a social worker vary from the polite 'it must be very interesting always meeting people, but isn't it exhausting?' to the Oxford don who confessed 'I know so little I can't even think what questions I should ask about it'. It is an understandable confusion due partly to the piecemeal development of social work services over the years, partly to the continued fragmentation of agencies and training plans. It is further confused by social workers' failure to be explicit about the essential nature of their job. We have 'not always avoided the pitfalls of making social work sound either esoteric or over-simple'.[1] Worse than that, it appears that there is often a conspiracy within the field to keep the public in the dark as to what it is all about.

[1] Ministry of Health *Report of the working party on social workers in the local authority health and welfare services* (Younghusband report) H.M.S.O., 1959, Section 15.

Problems and people

Social work today has a dual role. It is essential for social workers and social planners to be in continual interaction so that social policy for the community may be formed on the basis of known need. It is also the social worker's job to assess the nature and degree of trouble and to personalize social policy for the benefit of individuals and groups of people. The task may be to help them to adjust to changed circumstances, to accept stressful circumstances which cannot be altered, to improve poor personal or family relationships, or to regain confidence and self respect. Social work is popularly thought of as helping 'poor' people, that is people with little money, low intelligence or indifferent standards of cleanliness and morality. In fact the areas of social difficulty listed above are by no means confined to any income group or social class. The effects of impaired family relationships, 'difficult' children and habitual idleness may be mitigated by a comfortable bank balance. But money cannot solve all problems. As a recent 'pop' song has it 'money can't buy me love'; and the loneliness of the 'poor little rich girl' or the enforced dependence of a paralysed baronet may be just as much a matter for social help as the persistent truancy of a child with ragged clothes or the efforts of a harrassed mother to make ends meet.

The cause of social problems lies in the adverse inter-action of a person and his situation, his situation usually being the circumstances in which he lives and the people with whom he is in contact (his home and work, his family, friends, workmates and employers), and the circumstances of health, sickness, poverty or unhappiness which affect him. It is on the basis of situations that one of the classifications of social work is made. We speak of mentally and physically sick, handicapped, elderly, delinquent and unemployed people; of homeless families and 'problem' families; of children being maladjusted or 'at risk'. And social work agencies also tend to be organized along these lines.

Largely for this reason social workers are employed in a variety of statutory and voluntary organizations, some of which are set up principally to give a social work service, others, such as hospitals or courts, established primarily for a different purpose. The majority of social workers are in local or central government employment; others work in voluntary agencies, that is, those which are entirely supported by private subscription or partially State financed. Thus, medical and psychiatric social workers are employed by hospitals and clinics, probation officers are attached to courts and child care officers work in local authority Children's Departments. Local authority, health and welfare departments employ social workers of different kinds to help mentally and physically handicapped, mentally sub-normal, elderly and homeless people. Family caseworkers may work in the local authority or in voluntary organizations such as the Family Welfare Associations, Family Service Units, Guilds or Councils of Social Service and Old Peoples' Welfare Committees. Many voluntary agencies enlist the help of full or part-time volunteers. Most of these will undertake some form of in-service training to prepare for the job, and attend lectures run by university extra-mural departments where these are available. Volunteers who have not had a full training normally work under the guidance of a trained member of staff.

A further confusion in this field is caused by the indisciminate use of the words 'social work' and 'social welfare'. Social work is normally that carried out through the methods of casework, group work and community organization, while social welfare has a broader application to include the organization of the social services. There is, however, a general implication that a welfare officer is in some way inferior to a social worker, possibly because in the statutory social services and in the armed forces many welfare officers have had no formal training. The assumption that goes with this, however, that welfare is in its nature a less skilled occupation is a false one. The work of welfare officers in the local authority is extremely demanding, dealing as it does with the problems of severely and chronically sick people. The way in which a social problem is perceived will vary according to the organization offering help and the way in which a client presents his difficulty, but the focus of social work attention is always the client's need and the method of working will be basically the same. Differences in emphasis will be dictated by the special purpose of the agency; differences in the skill required lie rather in the complexity of the problem than in its social setting.

Training today

Whatever the field of employment, or specialization in preparing for the job, all social workers share a common area of knowledge and professional discipline. They must also be people who have the necessary personal qualities for sustained contact with situations of stress. People in trouble look for certain characteristics in the person from whom they ask help. They hope to find someone who will treat them seriously without being critical or shocked; who will respect their feelings and their confidence; who will assure them that help will be given without robbing them of their independence, and who will give them a feeling of security and worth. It goes without saying that workers must have real concern for people, warmth, integrity, tolerance, imagination and a sense of humour. Few people can offer all these qualities by nature although many have considerable intuitive ability to be helpful people. Training does not make the student a different person; it aims to foster or acquire the right qualities and to discipline the less useful ones as well as imparting knowledge. The task in training is to try to equip people to give help more effectively and surely: hit and miss methods are inadmissable when people's happiness is at stake.

For the most part the foundation for training in social work is laid in a university degree, diploma or certificate in social science in which the usual subjects are the pattern and administration of the social services, social history and economics, social psychology and an introduction to social work methods, with some practical experience in a variety of organizations. This is followed by a year of specialized training for the chosen field, either at a university, under the auspices of the Home Office (for probation and child care) or the Institute of Medical Social Work. An alternative is to take in this final year one of the university Applied Social Studies Courses which equip a student to practise in more than one field or to change fields after a period of supervised orientation.

In recent years different types of training have been recognized, notably in child care and probation, for older candidates with relevant experience. There are also now two year courses of training for the local authority health and welfare service and allied work run by colleges of further education.

In outline the basic study is of man, society and the interaction between them. The social worker aims to understand the problems of each person or groups of people; how they arose, why they cannot be dealt with unaided, why they are particularly troublesome at a point in time and what help can be given. To do this she needs to know something of normal human development and ways of behaving as the basis for assessing what seems to be abnormal in people's reactions to stressful situations; to realize the natural characteristics of man are to strive for independence and self respect, and that he has an innate capacity for growth and change. Although there are norms which may be expected and against which some evaluation of deviation may be made, each person is unique, so that each situation will be different and reaction to its stress or support will vary. This is especially important for a social worker to remember, because although she can never be in someone else's shoes or impose a solution on them she must try to understand what it means for them and so to help them work out their own solution or compromise.

Because stress, either from outside influence or from internal pressures, is the factor which precipitates most social problems it is necessary to learn something of the nature of social stress, with the object of understanding better why one person can tolerate seemingly unbearable conditions, whereas another is bowled over by them. The social work student also learns about the effect which the unconscious part of man's personality can have on his everyday life. This is particularly necessary in seeking to understand irrational behaviour—why for instance a person cannot take an apparently sensible course of action to get out of trouble, or why someone consistently gets into difficulty with the people in authority over him.

Social workers also learn from sociology about societies in different periods of history and of different cultures, of what internal and external factors influence the development of societies in different ways and of the causes of social groupings and social movements. This is applied to the study of present day society and the forces which affect development and change in attitudes towards political, social and cultural questions. People's beliefs, values and expectations are influenced by trends in contemporary society as well as by tradition, and this factor, too, the social worker must bear in mind in helping people to modify their environment or to live more in harmony with their surroundings.

Finally, a social worker learns about the social services, their origin, structure and function, so that she can work effectively within them, and help clients to use them appropriately.

Method

Skill in social work is normally acquired jointly in the theoretical application of knowledge to problem situations and in practical experience on the job under the guidance of a trained worker. This integration of theory and practice takes time. What seems simple on paper is apt to become quite a different matter when one is faced with a distressed or angry client or with a group of people who all talk at once or will not talk at all. The social worker learns that it is not enough to be sympathetic and eager to help; she must also know when to offer active help, when to encourage a man to do things for himself however long it takes, when to offer advice and when to do nothing but listen and try to understand. She must also try to be aware of the effect she has on her clients and of the subtle ways in which her own desires, inclinations and prejudices may intrude into the situation. The temptation to think we know best is strong in most of us, and the urge to give advice may not always be the right one.

Casework

Social work method, then, is essentially working *with* people, whether singly, in small groups or in the wider community. Work with one or two people is usually known as 'casework.' It is carried out through interviews in which client and worker seek to learn, to know and trust each other. The worker tries to understand what the problem is about and to assess the degree of distress and disruption it is causing. She can then consider what resources the client, his family or the community can offer to alleviate it. The client is given the chance to share his troubles, to clarify them through discussion, to seek information about sources of help and support in carrying out whatever plan they work out together. It is essentially a two way process. The social worker's skill lies in evaluating the situation accurately and acting appropriately; it is important to stimulate the client to find the solution which is acceptable to him and not to undermine his independence. The client needs to feel sure of the worker's genuine concern for him and of her willingness and ability to help.

Sometimes the problem is relatively simple and can be remedied by information about a service of which the client had no previous knowledge or by a direct grant of money. More often the position has become complex and overwhelming before the client has been forced to seek outside help; material and emotional factors may have become intricately entwined. When material help seems to be involved it is essential to try to understand what part it plays in the total situation; what meaning money or gifts have for the client and whether money is the real need or only a symptom of a wider problem. For example, Mrs Carter, the mother of a congenitally deformed child, asked a social work agency for the cost of the fare to the hospital where the baby was being cared for. She had not visited for some months and they were beginning to think she did not care. After discussion it seemed that Mrs Carter was indeed short of money and the fare was promised. Mrs Carter seemed loath to leave. The social worker had wondered if this was the whole trouble and indicated to Mrs Carter that having such a severely damaged child must be a great source of anxiety – perhaps visiting was a great strain on her. Mrs Carter admitted that she would do anything rather than visit; she couldn't bear to see the poor little mite like that – so helpless; she kept lying awake at night wondering if it was all her fault. She thought she could have scraped the money together, but the real trouble was that there was no-one she could talk to about it; her husband just shut up when she mentioned it and the neighbours seemed frightened of her now. She'd pretended to herself that if she didn't go to the hospital it would all turn out to be a bad dream. The social worker agreed that it was too much to cope with by herself and that it was only natural to be so upset. She offered to discuss it with Mrs Carter again after she had been to the hospital. Mrs Carter accepted, saying it made a world of difference to let off steam – the hospital wanted her to have the baby home soon and perhaps she and the social worker could talk about that; there was so much to think about and she'd have to help her husband and the children to know what to expect: she didn't think she could do that by herself.

In this situation the social worker had added to her sympathy for Mrs Carter her knowledge of the way in which people are liable to react to such tragic circumstances and the embarrassment which tends to alienate friends who would otherwise be the natural confidants. She knew, too, that it is often easier to approach an unknown agency with a concrete reason for help, such as money. Her tacit acknowledgement of this to Mrs Carter demonstrated her understanding of possible underlying distress and her willingness to talk about this if Mrs Carter thought it would be helpful. Had the worker simply given the fare money Mrs Carter would have remained unhappy until she found someone who did understand; worse, she might have felt that the interview confirmed her fears that she was in some way to blame and that this was a subject which she must keep to herself. As it was, she left assured that her concern for the baby was understood and better able to face the implications of having him home. It is the lessening of tension in this way that releases energy to cope with difficult material problems.

Some situations are the result of poor personal relationships. The trouble may be contained within a family, but the likelihood is that if it continues there will be repercussions outside. Family quarrels may lead the husband to be an inefficient employee, the wife to be careless about how the home is kept and the children to be distracted at school. Such were the Terrys. They did not want to split up, but could not see how to make things work. Their marriage had been fairly happy until they were rehoused in the suburbs away from Mrs Terry's mother.

Even after marriage Mrs Terry had depended on her mother to share responsibility for the daily care of the children, planning meals and baby sitting in the evenings. Now she resented the many demands of being a wife and mother; by the end of the day she was exhausted and bad tempered. Her husband openly said he was fed up with her: the home was no place to come back to and he couldn't understand what she did with the money. She was bewildered and miserable; he was disappointed and disillusioned. The situation did not change quickly, but over six months or so the Terrys went to the social worker either separately or together and gradually came to see what was wrong and how to put it right. They were really fond of each other and of the children, but they needed help in growing up to their responsibilities and to realize how much they needed each other. In a sense the social worker acted as a sounding board on which they could test out ideas which they could not have expressed on their own.

Group work

Group work is the term usually applied to working with a small group of people. For example, it might be a family, a club, a committee or a collection of people working on some project. It is also a way of working being used increasingly to help those with similar difficulties to help each other. It might, for instance, be groups of parents of delinquent children, of people learning to live with handicaps or of people nearing retirement age. The basic knowledge required is the same as for casework in studying personality make-up and personal relationships, but here the emphasis is on the interplay of the members of the group and of the role cast and accepted for each member of the group. The aim is that the group shall work steadily towards performing the task which it has taken on or which falls to it. The social worker's job is to enable this to happen. This implies that as well as being aware of the nature of the one-to-one relationship between herself and any member she must be alert to all the cross currents in relationships.

She needs constantly to assess what the group is doing, what is promoting or impeding progress and, if necessary, to interpret to the group what she sees as taking place. This method of working often reflects in a purposeful and knowledgeable way situations which are common to daily experience. Everyone is a member of numerous groups from the family onwards, the family being the basic group in our society, and usually the pattern for other groups. Ability to work productively in a group can be translated from one situation to another. It is also a means of sharing common difficulties and of gaining support from others with similar experience in learning to live with a situation which cannot be changed.

Group work is a method which is frequently used to help members of a family – for instance, to communicate more freely. To take an example: in the McKay family the tradition was one of sturdy individualism: the children were brought up to stand on their own feet. They were a proud family in which success was important and weakness frowned upon. When Helen, at 17, became illegitimately pregnant they were horrified and baffled. Dr and Mrs McKay were affectionate but undemonstrative. In their shame and distress they became less able to communicate, even on practical measures. Each parent secretly blamed the other, both blamed the school and the youth club. Dr McKay wanted to disown Helen; his wife fought to keep her. Coming into the home the social worker found she had almost to introduce the members of the family to each other; they were figures going their own ways rather than real people sharing a common life. They could talk to her as someone anonymous but concerned, and gradually began to talk meaningfully to each other. They needed help in learning to share their feelings of failure as well as success before they could work together to help Helen. The easier relationships which finally resulted made their family life firmer than it had been before.

Results

The results of social work intervention are difficult to measure, but increasingly social workers are aware of the need to demonstrate in what ways this method of helping can be effective. They are frequently challenged by the question 'is your service a luxury or a necessity?' If adequate funds are to be allocated the question must be answered convincingly. Statistics of numbers of clients applying to agencies or totals of monies paid out are no proof of effectiveness; they are a measurement of activity. The real value of social work is seen in the extent to which people who have been offered this kind of help are living as happier and more useful citizens. It will always be argued that this improvement might have come about for a variety of reasons, and it is true that social work would not claim a monopoly among the helping professions. But systematic documentation of results claimed from social work help, in terms as clearly visible to the community as to the social work profession, could provide both proof of worth and a clearer picture of what social work is. If the results of work in the cases outlined in this chapter were assessed it could be claimed that Mrs Carter was able to visit her baby with less misery than before and begin plans to accept him into the family – one child saved from a life of institutional care.

The social workers

Mr and Mrs Terry's marriage was established on a more mature footing – one broken home the fewer. Dr and Mrs McKay were able to rebuild their family life on a more protective basis and to accept their unexpected grandchild – one illegitimate baby retained within a family setting.

Even when the case is established, however, it is argued that a service of this kind needs resources of money and personnel that are not readily forthcoming. Not only social work but the allied fields of teaching, medicine and nursing are short of workers, indeed are competing for recruits. It becomes increasingly important, therefore, for social work to consider whether its organization and methods are as economic and efficient as they should be.

The fragmentation referred to earlier is a continuing reproach and the need for better co-operation and joint endeavour is constantly being urged. Logically, there should be no reason against a great deal more amalgamation of services; even within the statutory services legislation could be promoted to facilitate more co-ordination of effort. But the traditional pattern is hard to change and the profession of social work too newly emerging to feel secure in raising a common voice on the best use of available resources.

Changes

There are signs of change. Discussions among the professional organizations about a joint association for social workers of all branches have led to a greater measure of understanding of the common ground and of the differences between the various sections. With increased understanding of group interaction we may hope before too long for better communication and co-operation between social workers and social work agencies. The instances of six or seven workers visiting the same family are already fewer than five years ago, but effective co-operation at this level can only be based on the acceptance of commonly held aim, and principles.

One way of achieving this is by making the essential elements in training available to more people. A start has been made but perhaps an even bolder plan needs to be evolved to ensure more evenness in practice and therefore more interchange between workers. There is no better way of learning to co-operate than in working together, however painful may be the growing pains.

It is not, however, only for reasons of effective deployment and administrative convenience that co-ordination is necessary. There are still people whose needs are not provided for in spite of our comprehensive services.

Although we recognize the need for prevention some people still only become eligible for help after trouble has set in. Much publicity is given to the question of teenage troubles, but the worried parents of a turbulent adolescent may get their first chance of help after trouble has brought their child to court. Many lonely people who see no purpose in life have been discovered since the Samaritan telephone service began, but too many people are only brought within the official scope of social help after a suicide attempt has landed them in hospital. Because social work is still seen as primarily for the under-privileged, professional and financially secure people are hesitant to approach a social work agency – it is not respectable. Usually they see their only source of help in personal problems in psychiatry, an expensive remedy and not always appropriate.

There is a good deal of interest in some quarters in providing a comprehensive family service. The need for this is undoubted. In one move it could promote a more effective and economic means of help to a wider range of people, and it should make for streamlining of staff, time and effort. It can only work, however, if the intention is to see the needs of the family as a whole and to cease to view them as a series of specializations. The greatest need in social work today is for practical recognition that man is a person, not a problem. The emphasis must shift from classifying situations to considering how better to help the people in them. Intellectual recognition of this is implicit in the content of social work training. It is the practical application which still lags behind the theory.

Family welfare

A. FREDERICK PHILP

A great deal of social work inevitably touches on family life, and in this essay Frederick Philp, National Secretary of the Family Service Units, assesses the range of welfare provided for the family.

Mr Philp was formerly Training Officer and Leader of the Liverpool Family Service Unit. He is on the Management Committee of the Family Centre of Hackney, Stoke Newington, and a member of the Executive Committee of the National Bureau for Co-operation in Child Care. He is author of *Family failure* (1963) and joint author with Noel Timms of *The problem of 'the problem family'* (1957).

Our ability to enter into social relationships and our expectation of them is conditioned by previous experiences; and normally the first experience of relationships is gained within the family.

Here, in his earliest years, the child makes close attachments to his mother and father and as his desires are satisfied and inevitably at times frustrated, he experiences a range of feeling towards those nearest to him and on whom he is most dependent. Within the family circle he has a variety of relationships – with mother and father, brothers and sisters, grandparents and family friends. As he develops and his needs change, new balances are achieved between his dependence on others within the family and his need to find himself and be independent of them. In the family he learns the give and take of relationships, learns to enjoy himself and give pleasure to others, to control his anger and use his aggressive impulses constructively.

Where the family can satisfy his needs appropriately as he grows up, he is able to move off on independent explorations and return for the support and affection he still needs. So he adds to his experience of relationships through new contacts in play, at school and at work. Eventually, he can appreciate his home in the context of his wider experience of relationships; he becomes able to see his parents and brothers and sisters more realistically whereas formerly his vision was coloured by his dependency and the strong feelings accompanying it. So he becomes able to live his own life with a different kind of attachment to his family of origin. He can find satisfaction in his work or in what he is able to do with his earnings; he can establish his own home and derive satisfaction from sexual relationships, parenthood and the inter-dependence of marriage.

Man has a great capacity for adaptation and recovery and can overcome very severe handicaps; but, when things go wrong in important relationships early in life, there are long-term effects. Hurts and angry feelings, resentments, which could never be worked out with the parents with whom they first arose, may be taken quite inappropriately into relationships in later life.

A child may feel responsible for the loss of a parent and all that happens subsequently may seem to confirm his guilt; such feelings and fantasies may make it hard for him to find satisfaction in close relationships, to cope with illness reasonably or feel secure in dealing with his own children.

Difficulties which arise later in life often reawaken feelings related to past disappointments and childhood relationships and, within the family, the unhappiness or problem of one member has repercussions on others. The family really is a network of relationships, not a constellation of static objects. A pull on one member is transmitted to others through the links between them. An old adage says that 'misfortunes seldom come single' and social workers frequently see this demonstrated in families. A mother's illness makes it more difficult for her to do everything she did formerly and she is more preoccupied with herself. Because she is less responsive to the children, they become more difficult to manage; unsettled at home, they do less well at school and so bring new demands on the parents from teachers and others outside the home. The father, already anxious about his wife, receives less comfort from the home and may be less able to work. His earnings fall and he looks for satisfactions outside the home. What starts as the illness of one member grows into a complex of family problems. Fortunately, in most families, other factors enter to prevent this kind of decline but sometimes the intervention of a social worker is needed to give constructive forces a chance to operate.

A good home provides security and stimulation for growing children but it is not a place of constant calm where the family members collude to avoid emotional upsets or where there are no difficulties to be overcome. The sense of security derives from family relationships which can tolerate a range of feeling without disruption and can adapt to the changing needs of family members.

The family meets many natural stresses requiring readjustments. Time and the process of ageing bring changes in themselves; parents find that certain tasks become more difficult and take longer. The birth of a new baby makes many demands for change on both parents and older children. Illness can test the parents' emotional balance, can entail changes of income and occupation and changed expectations within the family. Contacts with old people may enrich the children's experience but responsibilities towards ageing grandparents may bring additional stress to the family. Death with all its emotional and material repercussions may occur at any time.

General family services

Family welfare can be considered to have two aspects

The social workers

Firstly, as a general policy of support for the family through social services so that parents may be helped to establish the basic conditions for good family life. Secondly, we may consider it as a service given by social workers to families who are finding difficulty in meeting some problem which has arisen for them and who need assistance from someone outside the family circle.

The statutory services should provide a general background of security for the family so that it is not disrupted by external pressures over which it has no control but is helped to weather the ordinary difficulties of everyday life. An income to enable the parents to meet the family's needs, accommodation and care in sickness – these are all of primary importance.

Before the War one might well have said that the most important requirement for family welfare was that the father should have opportunity to work. Now we have almost come to take full employment for granted, but is is this perhaps which has meant the most substantial change in life in recent years.

A regular wage has brought with it changes in home comfort and in expectations for children, a greater freedom to enjoy family and social relationships. The Ministry of Labour's services for disabled persons have made regular employment possible for many handicapped people. For those without work or unable to work because of illness the system of national insurance and national assistance provides a regular income. Child allowances for the income tax payer and family allowances help to increase the income of those with dependent children.

All these provisions have made a considerable contribution to the welfare of families but, in many respects, the situation is unsatisfactory. The income tax allowances for children make little difference to low wage earners but give a substantial additional income to the better-off. Family allowances are important to families with several children and a low income, but the amount of the allowances (8/- for the second child and 10/- for the third and subsequent children) has not changed since 1956 and they have never provided the help they were designed to give when recommended in the Beveridge Report. To give family allowances which would be the same proportion of average earnings as those Beveridge recommended would now mean an allowance of about 32/- a week per child.

Moreover, there are still many poor families in our prosperous and 'affluent' society. In 1963 the National Assistance Board estimated that they were assisting 100,000 children in families where the income was less than the N.A.B. scales for the needs of a family of that composition. It has been estimated that at least as many, and perhaps three times as many children are living in wage earner's families at a similar level of income without the help of National Assistance. In this situation something is seriously wrong, and we must expect to pay for their present deprivation in their poor health, low productivity and demands on the social services in later life.

Public attention has been drawn recently to London's housing problems. In many parts of the country families are having to manage in accommodation which is overcrowded, structurally unsatisfactory and lacking in domestic facilities; many families are paying rent beyond their means for a roof over their heads and in London some are homeless because, despite their readiness to pay and their efforts to find accommodation, they can find no accommodation to rent. Housing shortage is, above all, a family problem, for parents with young children are at a disadvantage; they do not have the freedom to look around and the needs of dependent children limits what they can pay in rent; many are forced by their need of immediate shelter into unsatisfactory accommodation.

It is perhaps necessary to think afresh about the provision we are prepared to make for the welfare of families and children in our society. Should the family with dependent children be given additional help with housing? Should we not give larger family allowances and do away with the income tax allowances for children?

The National Health Service is one of the major measures for the welfare of families. Illness comes to us all at some time and it is most important for parents to be able to obtain medical and dental care for themselves and their children without anxiety about the cost. But the local health service may be as important to the family as the treatment they receive from general practitioner, dentist and hospital. This provides among other things: ante and post-natal care; the infant welfare centres and health visiting service; a vaccination and diphtheria immunization service; the midwifery and home nursing service; and the home help service which gives domestic assistance in the home during a mother's illness or confinement. In addition there is the attention given to children's health and welfare by the school medical service.

It would be wrong to leave these general services without reference to education. Local authorities provide a range of services for children with special needs. These who show problems at school may be helped through child guidance services or through a special educational provision in schools for physically handicapped, educationally subnormal or maladjusted children. School meals make a valuable contribution to the feeding of the growing child and to the family budget. The Youth Employment Service advises school leavers on finding work and the Youth Service supports recreational and social activities of young people outside school. Welfare workers from the Education Department assist parents whose children are handicapped or whose income makes it difficult for them to meet the school child's needs fully.

Home and parent

Good co-operation between home and school is necessary if a child is to obtain full benefit from the education system but the interest shown by schools in the home circumstances of their children varies greatly. In many cases the task of establishing better co-operation between home and school is left to the school welfare service; but this, though the oldest of the local authority social services, is the least well-developed. It should be one of the most important social work services, recognizing incipient difficulties in school children, fostering mutual understanding and co-operation between home and school, and using the range of special educational provisions – nursery schools, boarding schools, special schools – to help children where there are family problems. Unfortunately, in recent years, the education welfare service has not been as attractive to trained social workers as other local authority services have and we seem to be losing the opportunity of bringing highly skilled social work to the service of schools, children and families when problems first appear.

One group of families, above all, needs more help in the future than it has received hitherto, namely, single parent families. The group includes widows and widowers and their children, separated and divorced parents with their children and unmarried mothers and their families. These people are in very different situations but in all cases one parent is bearing alone the responsibility of the family and attempting to meet the children's needs. The fact that there have always been women who have had to bring up their children alone and that many have done so very successfully must not make us ignore the difficulties. The burden is possibly greater in any case in a society where higher standards of living and greater material comfort is expected by everyone, where most people are married and where help is less readily available from grandparents and relatives. The single parent family is generally at a disadvantage financially; those who work have additional expenses in making provision for their children while they do so; a man with children usually has to obtain paid domestic help. Tax allowances give little recognition to the extra burden of managing alone. But the problems are not only financial; the school holidays are a problem for those who have to work; there is no respite from the responsibility of being the one parent, every decision concerning the children has to be taken by one person. Many of these difficulties cannot be avoided but the burden could often be eased if there were a readier recognition of the stresses of the situation regardless of the circumstances in which the absent parent was lost.

Family casework

This framework of good general social services which can support the family in the community is the foundation of a policy of family welfare. These services need to be supplemented by the personal social work services – family casework services which will help families with special difficulties. Some of these (and an increasing number) may be provided by the statutory bodies, but the majority are still voluntary agencies employing trained social workers (as for example the Family Welfare Association and Family Service Units).

The voluntary societies in the past received many requests for help in financial difficulties and with problems in relation to employment, sickness and education, matters in which more provision is now made by the statutory services. The family caseworker still deals with special difficulties in all these areas but her help is increasingly sought by people who feel that their problem is one of family relationships – or, even, is a difficulty within themselves – and who want help to understand what has gone wrong and to see how things might change.

Mr and Mrs Z. were intelligent and capable parents but faced a family problem they could not deal with alone. They were immigrants from Northern Europe and had not been in England for very long. Mrs Z. felt isolated and uprooted and spoke very broken English. Their problem concerned the elder of their two children, a boy with a severe congenital disability who had been in hospital for long periods and had recently been discharged home. Shortly after his return Mrs Z. found she was pregnant. She became extremely anxious, afraid that she might give birth to another handicapped child and doubtful of her ability to look after the elder child adequately. She felt overwhelmed by the demands on her and her anxious state created some friction within the marriage.

The caseworker saw the parents frequently in their home during the difficult period. As they talked over their worries, the parents came to feel that it would be best for the handicapped child to be placed in a special boarding school, and the caseworker helped them to find a suitable school.

The new baby was a perfectly healthy and well-formed child and following his birth the tension in the home decreased. The mother was happier in herself and able to respond with more confidence and spontaneity to her husband and children. With greater confidence in herself and evidence of her ability to manage, her command of English began to improve. The handicapped child came home for the holidays and the parents visited and kept in touch with him during term time. They felt that he was gaining much from the school and that their decision had been the right one for him, not a rejection about which they need feel ashamed. They looked forward to the possibility of his eventual return to the home when he had been able to profit from the special schooling and they were able to look after him.

These parents were capable people with high standards of child care and personal behaviour. Faced with the demands of a severely handicapped child in a strange country without the support of relatives they needed help at a time of crisis. But much family casework nowadays is with families where the level of home and child care is low and there is a danger that the family will break up or the children suffer neglect unless substantial help can be given. These families present many problems to the social services. There is often financial mismanagement, with debts, rent arrears, threats of eviction and Court orders. The children may be poorly fed, clad and cared for, and the home barren and neglected. The father may show little interest in the home and children, work irregularly and fail to provide adequately for the family's needs.

There is often marital strife. The children may be emotionally disturbed or out of control, doing badly at school or at work. Because of the number and persistence of their problems, these families are often referred to as 'problem families'.

Concentration on the problems these families present to the welfare services may blind us to the disabilities and needs of the people concerned. The families are often large and their income low. The parents are handicapped by physical and mental ill-health, by lack of education, training and industrial skill and, above all, by their own home backgrounds, and earlier experiences. Pressures to change their way of life tend to add to their problems. It is only when they can feel differently about themselves and their families that improvement can take place.

When referred for help to a family agency Mr and Mrs A. had six children and were expecting another. There had been contacts with several social services previously but with little effect. The letter of referral spoke of dirty conditions and poor home management; the father had been unemployed for at least three years; the children were not developing very well and the mother had sought advice about them from the hospital on several occasions.

Mrs A. was at first very reluctant to have the family caseworker visit her because she was afraid that she might take over the management of the home and income. When the hospital doctor explained that this was not what the contact would be like, she accepted it saying that it would give her more encouragement to keep the home in order if someone were coming to see her.

On the first contact and for several weeks after, Mrs A. kept everything securely under her control and showed the worker, by her actions as well as in what she said, how much she felt she had to be responsible for everything that happened to the family. She felt that it was all too great a burden for her, but no-one could help her; other people would only criticize and expect more from her. Mr A. remained in the background, seeing the worker for a few minutes at first and on one occasion in his wife's absence commenting on how impossible it was to do anything to help her.

Gradually, in the course of weekly contacts, the mother gained growing confidence that the worker was genuinely concerned for her and wished to see her succeed as a mother. Mr and Mrs A. became more able to talk to one another about their difficulties. They planned together for the coming confinement, cleared off the rent arrears and prepared to find better accommodation. Mrs A. started to seek the worker's advice on the care of the baby and the management of the older children. She felt able to use the infant welfare centre and invite other people into her home. As she became less anxious and more confident in herself she could allow more freedom and independence to those around her; the baby was 'the easiest she had ever had'; the children did much better at school and Mr A. was able to seek work.

As she gained the mother's confidence the worker learned how in childhood Mrs A. had felt inferior to her brothers and sisters and had been dominated by her mother who had expected very little of her. The marriage had occurred largely in defiance of her mother and she had felt that a constant superhuman effort was needed if

51

she were not to fail as her mother expected her to do. The caseworker's understanding of her feelings and background enabled her to help Mrs A. to become a more confident, relaxed and capable mother. Without this sensitive appreciation of the family interaction it would have been very easy for her to try to bring about changes too rapidly and so seem to Mrs A. to present her again with the mother-daughter relationship about which she felt so much resentment.

Work with families with such long-standing problems may need to go on for several years. In fact, some families will always need support from the social services if they are to provide a reasonable home for their children. What is actually done for them may be slight but they may need to feel that how they are managing matters to someone outside the home, and an occasional contact with a social worker who has helped them in the past may give them the continuing encouragement they need.

During recent years there has been a great increase in the family casework undertaken by local authorities as they have been more and more concerned to help families who might otherwise become homeless or whose children might have to be taken into children's homes. In different parts of the country this work has been carried on by specially appointed social workers in health, children's welfare and education departments and, in a few cases (e.g. Hertfordshire), in specially created Family Welfare Departments. The Children and Young Persons Act, 1963, laid a duty on local authorities to make available advice, guidance and assistance to prevent children coming into or remaining in care or coming before a juvenile court. Since then many Children's Departments have appointed family caseworkers to their staff and further appointments will be made in coming years. This preventive work is a development of the main function of a Children's Department in providing foster homes and institutional care for children deprived temporarily or permanently of a normal home life.

Training

Training in family casework is provided primarily by voluntary bodies. The principle organizations are the Family Welfare Association in London, the direct descendant of the Charity Organization Society; the Invalid Children's Aid Association, which works with families where there is a sick or handicapped child; and Family Service Units which anticipated the legislation referred to above and has since 1947 provided a service for families whose many problems jeopardized the welfare of the children. In several provincial cities there are smaller organizations which have given family casework services of high quality for many years. These organizations take social work students for periods of practical experience in a family casework setting and provide field work supervision for university students taking professional training in Applied Social Studies courses and wishing to qualify as family caseworkers.

It should, perhaps, be repeated that nowadays 'voluntary organization' does not imply that there are many unpaid workers. The voluntary family casework bodies are staffed by full-time professional staff whose salaries and conditions of service are similar to their colleagues in the statutory services.

Conserving resources

The voluntary bodies meet similar problems both organizationally and in their work and could perhaps benefit from sharing their experience with one another. With this in mind, Family Service Units, the Family Welfare Association and the Invalid Children's Aid Association with the financial support of the London Parochial Charities, in 1963 established the Family Centre of Hackney and Stoke Newington. Each of the three bodies takes part in the management and staffing of the Centre which provides within one administrative Unit the casework services elsewhere provided by the three organizations separately. It will operate for an initial experimental period of five years and it is hoped that in this time the bodies concerned will be able to assess the casework needs of the area and see what benefits comes from the combined operation.

In a number of other areas of the country arrangements are being made for voluntary bodies to share premises so that several services may be readily available to families. On some new housing areas there are centres where social workers from both statutory services and voluntary bodies can have offices; such arrangements facilitate co-operation and make help more readily available to those in need. In some of our large cities a troubled family has sometimes undertaken a long journey to a big central office of a social service department only to be referred on to a more appropriate service in another central office some distance away. Such experiences can make it more difficult for families to use the help available.

One of the suggestions of the Ingleby Committee (1960) on the law relating to Children and Young Persons[1] was that local authorities might establish Family Advice Centres which would serve as central reference points for members of the public in need of advice or assistance on the welfare of their children. Local authorities were not required to establish such Centres by the Children and Young Persons Act 1963 but with the encouragement of the Home Office many are now doing so. The concept of these Centres has been explained in the report of the Longford Committee.[2]

[1] Home Office *Report of the Committee on Children and Young Persons* (Ingleby Committee) H.M.S.O., 1960, Cmnd. 1191.

[2] *Crime – a challenge to us all;* report of the Labour Party's Study Group (Longford Report) Labour Party, 1964.

They should be cheerful, attractive places and should serve families with all kinds of problems; voluntary organizations as well as statutory services will use them. Their function will be to provide factual advice where this is needed, to put people in touch with the appropriate services when the problems are relatively straightforward and to arrange appointments with specialist workers who can deal with the more complicated problems. Such Centres, if they come to be highly regarded by the general public, could enable assistance to be given at an early stage of difficulty and so make an important contribution to family welfare; but it is clear that they need staff of high calibre, social workers to whom disturbed and diffident callers can talk about their personal affairs and who can assess rapidly the extent of the difficulties and respond accordingly.

The growth of the social services has meant that where there are many problems, many services may be concerned with one family. This is not only wasteful of scarce resources; it may be harmful to the family if they receive conflicting advice or are able to play one service against another. To encourage co-operation and prevent overlapping, co-ordinating committees are in existence in most areas.

Increasingly, however, doubt is being expressed as to whether co-ordination of this kind is enough. Is it not desirable to have a local authority Family Service which will combine in one department the major services concerned with children and family welfare? The McBoyle Committee (1963)[1] on the prevention of neglect of children in Scotland commented: 'A comprehensive family service would help to avoid the overlapping and omissions which result from the present arrangements. It would facilitate the continuity and unity which are

[1] Scottish Advisory Council on Child Care *Prevention of neglect of children*: report of the (McBoyle) Committee. H.M.S.O., 1963, Cmnd. 1966.

fundamental to effective social work and make possible the best and most effective use of the trained field workers whose numbers are still comparatively small.'

The most detailed proposals so far have been made in the report of a Study Group on Crime appointed by the Labour Party under the Chairmanship of Lord Longford.[1] This Committee recommended the establishment of a Family Service under the central direction of the Home Office and with Family Service Committees of local authorities to administer Family Service Departments.

The Service would incorporate the present children's departments and parts of health, education and welfare departments. It would be concerned with homeless families, handicapped, neglected and deprived children, unmarried mothers and their children and would have as one of its main tasks 'to advise, guide and generally promote the welfare of families and of children and young people up to the age of 18'.

Will a unified family welfare service of this kind be established and if so how quickly? The arguments for such a reorganization are very strong but it cannot be carried through without considerable disruption of the present system.

The answer may depend largely on financial factors but economy at the expense of child welfare can be false economy which is paid for dearly later on. If we had an effective service of research as a built-in part of our social services we should probably be able to demonstrate the truth of that proposition without question. The pioneers of social casework believed that a sound assessment of the case should precede treatment but in dealing with human problems we cannot always operate in such a logical way. We can, however, avoid acting blindly and we must try to see that in future practice, research and training keep more closely in step with one another.

[1] *Crime – a challenge to us all, op. cit.*

Work in the community

MURIEL A. SMITH

Work in the community includes some of the oldest and newest approaches to social work. In the cities, residential settlements have often been serving local needs for half a century or longer. More recently the emphasis has widened to include work with other local groups and the social development of new towns and housing projects. As this kind of work extends and ramifies, the problem of terminology becomes more difficult. In this paper Muriel Smith adopts distinctive terms for different kinds of community work: 'community development,' 'community organization,' 'social development.' She does so not because she believes there is general agreement about this usage, but merely to offer a framework that further discussion may refine and clarify.

Muriel Smith is a Community Development Officer of the London Council of Social Service. She initially took a philosophy degree at Reading University, but trained for social work at Liverpool during the war. She has done youth work in Liverpool, and elsewhere and was Assistant Warden of a Community Centre in Reading, before joining the London Council of Social Service in 1949. She is also a member of the Central Housing Advisory Committee.

The word 'community' is almost impossible to define satisfactorily. One American sociologist lists over 100 definitions. Most of these include some reference to a geographical area and to a subjective 'feeling of belonging'. The feeling of belonging to a community is not necessarily related to any geographical area, but is one way of describing a network of personal and group relationships. It is in the sense of a local community that the word is most often used in what follows, and the phrase 'work in the community' is used for the sake of convenience to cover several different ways of working either with small groups or local communities.

The anthropologist might be able to discern different degrees of community. At one end of the scale there is the isolated, tight-knit, integrated community, which gives maximum security but is restrictive, narrow and lacking in opportunity for its young people. It would be difficult to find an extreme example in this country, but one would look for it in some remote village or island. At the other end there is the geographical community in which people are not united by common beliefs, customs, aspirations and relationships. This is the community that is so new that few people know one another, as in some new housing developments, or so large that the individual feels lost and of no significance, as for example the bed-sitter population of a west London district. In fact these are not communities at all.

If we try to make value judgments about what is a good community, most people would agree that it is neither of these two extremes, but would disagree on where the balance lies between them.

Historical development

Historically, it was industrialization and urbanization that created the evil conditions of the eighteenth and nineteenth centuries, in which community work and youth work (which is one form of working with groups) became a necessity. Today technological change is always bringing new social problems, but with greatly improved social conditions the emphasis is not so much on the needs of deprived districts and the problems of social breakdown, however serious, as on the creation of a social environment which gives support to those in difficulty and prevents such problems from arising.

SETTLEMENT WORKERS. In 1873 Canon Barnett settled in Whitechapel as vicar of a parish in east London, and started a residential settlement known as Toynbee Hall. This was the first of a number of residential settlements in the overcrowded areas of large cities. Young men and women, many of them graduates from well-to-do families, volunteered to live in the Settlement House, carry on their professions, and give their free time to improving conditions for their neighbours.

This they did in three ways. First they tried to influence legislation and to get their friends in high places to take political action. Secondly they influenced public opinion by writing articles and making speeches; they wrote to their friends asking for money, clothing and other forms of help; and they invited them to sit on management committees and to come and see for themselves what conditions were like. Thirdly, they gave relief and practical help to those around who came into the settlements for recreation or relief. Lord Beveridge, William Temple, and Lord Attlee, all spent some time as young men living in a residential settlement.

This was the age when many of the youth organizations and clubs were started in an attempt to give children and young people a place to go which catered for their general welfare as well as their recreational needs, and the settlements organized youth clubs of their own. Thus youth organizations in this country, unlike some of the youth movements on the Continent organized by young people themselves, were the result of adults whose social conscience had been aroused.

Today many settlements are still making a contribution to the welfare of the community around them, but some are wondering what their future role will be. Many have large buildings, which are a considerable drain on their resources. Some of the residents are university students, often with very much less money and time than the young people in the clubs whom they are still trying to help. In many settlements there has been a change of emphasis. One at Blackfriars in London, has concentrated on the needs of discharged prisoners, another in Manchester on play schemes for children. A London University Settlement provides a club for the parents of ineducable children. One in Bermondsey has sold its buildings to provide the money for workers on a new estate; and still another in Bristol has made a detailed study of the process of slum clearance and rehousing that went on around their building.

COMMUNITY CENTRES AND COMMUNITY ASSOCIATIONS. A new development between the wars, in which the National Council of Social Service played a considerable part, was the setting up of community associations and centres on new estates outside some of the large cities. Among the first were the Watling Community Centre, at Edgware, Middlesex, and centres at Manchester and Sheffield. These estates were often the result of early rehousing programmes. They had few amenities, and people felt cut off from friends and relatives. The community associations aimed to bring together individuals and local branches of national voluntary organizations, as well as the churches and political parties. In addition the association might form interest groups of its own for drama, discussion, sports or music. It was hoped that these associations would take a special interest in the general welfare of the neighbourhood and manage a community centre, a building which they could all share. Many of these associations started spontaneously and helped to create friendly relationships among strangers.

Although the first community centres were built with money from voluntary sources, the Board of Education, (as it then was) became interested, and grant-aid for community centres was available under the Physical Training and Recreation Act 1937, the Housing Act 1936, and the Education Act 1944. Local authorities were able to build community centres, employ a warden and if necessary maintain the centre, but it was still managed by a voluntary organization – the community association. Under the Education Acts authorities only made provision where genuine local interest had been shown. Local education authorities should assess community associations not so much by the number of educational activities they sponsor as their sensitivity and response to local problems and needs. The Ministry of Education issued a Red Book with plans for community centres showing adequate accommodation for several different activities to take place at one time. Owing, however, to the fact that community centres were a very low priority on the education budget, most areas had to be content with very modest buildings, if they were lucky enough to get one at all. Some community centres (for example in Bristol) were built with voluntary labour.

Community associations are not confined to new housing areas, and in the post-war period took root in suburban districts, in small towns, and in large cities. Some education authorities employ wardens; others grant-aid the association to appoint its own secretary-warden.

There is a National Federation of Community Associations which works in association with the National Council of Social Service and receives grants from the Department of State for Education and Science. It provides advice and information on all aspects of community association work. It has travelling officers in three regions of England, and there is an officer responsible for community work in the Council of Social Service office in Scotland and Wales. There are about 440 members apart from individuals, including eighteen local authorities and development corporations. Community associations are fairly evenly spread in the north, the south, and the Midlands.

One difference between the residential settlement and the community centre is that the secretary of the community association carries out the policy of the association, which is composed of representatives of local organizations and local people, while the warden of the residential settlement is responsible to a management committee or council composed of people who in general live outside the area. A happy relationship sometimes exists when the settlement provides the accommodation for the community association, and itself carries on specific pieces of social work alongside.

There has sometimes been a rather too rigid distinction between the community centre, which the local education authority has regarded as 'adult education', and the youth centre or youth club, which has been regarded as separate from it and coming under the 'service of youth'. Although separate buildings may be desirable because of noise and the nature of the activities, young people need to be encouraged to feel part of the adult community and should not be deliberately excluded from adult recreation and interests.

The provision of youth services is a partnership between statutory and voluntary organizations in an attempt to provide young people with opportunities to develop their interests, make satisfactory personal relationships and enjoy their leisure as members of a group. In 1939 the Board of Education issued circular 1486 *In the service of youth*, which suggested ways in which the local education authority and voluntary organizations could become partners in providing facilities and opportunities for young people in their leisure time. This circular was mainly concerned with the 14–18 age group. The present Development Council of the Department of Education and Science is mainly concerned with the 14-21 age group, and there is an urgent need for more consideration to be given to the leisure-time needs of the under 14's, along the lines of the report – *Out of school*, by the Central Advisory Council for Education.

Work in the community

In Circular 1486 local authorities were urged to set up youth committees and to appoint county and borough youth organizers. Money was made available to the voluntary organizations to improve their buildings and to employ more staff. National organizations such as the National Association of Boys' Clubs, the National Association of Youth Clubs, the Y.W.C.A. and the Y.M.C.A. co-operated with the Government, and in addition new pre-service organizations were formed, which attracted many young people who wanted to do something to serve the community during the war.

Where there were obvious gaps in the provision of youth clubs the Borough Youth Committee sometimes recommended the local education authority to make direct provision of youth centres and clubs. Some authorities were much more enterprising than others. Where both the voluntary organization and the local authority have strong policies, the results appeared more satisfactory than where one partner is weak and the other strong.

COMMUNITY DEVELOPMENT. The idea of the residential settlement spread from London to the rest of the country, and was taken up in the U.S., where there are a number of settlements and neighbourhood houses, and from there to other parts of the world. Community centres have been provided in urban areas in some of the developing countries. These are ideas which have been exported. Community *development* on the other hand has to a large extent been imported from developing countries.

Community development may mean many different things. It may be used in a developing country as an umbrella term to cover economic and social development, of which social welfare programmes are only a small part; but it may also be used to describe a local project, for example, the building of a school or a clinic by local people, with the help of Government resources.

In a developing country there may be a team of experts concerned with health, agriculture, education and so on. In this team there is a place for the community development worker who has no special responsibility except to assist the local people. His job is not to put over government policy, but to get to know people in the local village well enough to help them express what they believe to be ways of improving their conditions. In other words, he seeks to help people to achieve their own goals and does not come with his mind made up on what is best for them.

Although the local community may not decide on a project which he thinks important, he assists them, knowing that when people co-operate and achieve something they want, they soon look around to discover what task ought to be tackled next. The community development worker is primarily concerned with people and must know enough about community resources to help them achieve their objectives. The specialist in the team may be responsible primarily for health, agriculture or education, but as an administrator he will not get very far unless he too knows how to work with people. He therefore needs skills in human relations in the same way as the community development worker.

There are now people working in the same way in this country. They are not so much concerned with helping people meet their primary needs, which are looked after by central or local Government; the problems of a developed country are much less tangible. These people work with a number of independent groups which have their own objectives, make their own policy and organize their own activities. It is not surprising that with improved social conditions, better education and opportunities, more people are interested in running their own affairs and no longer feel the need for professional workers or volunteers from other parts of the country to come and organize clubs for them.

Leadership of voluntary organizations has often in the past been in the hands of middle-class people, but there is more indigenous leadership than is often recognized. The community development worker is an 'enabler', a detached helper who works with an autonomous group. Such a worker can be described as a 'detached' community worker, because although he must have the security of a social agency or a local authority which employs and supports him, the policy of the agency or authority must be, within a very broad framework, to help the community achieve its own ends. He can work in many different settings. In the blocks of flats in London and other cities there are tenants' associations and social clubs meeting in some cases in clubrooms provided by the Local Housing Authority. Many of the organizations in London have a well-developed programme of social activities; they organize youth sections, and clubs for elderly people; they run outings and parties at Christmas. They co-operate with the local authority over welfare matters that concern all the residents, such as the need for a children's play area, and make a channel of communication with the landlord. They encourage friendly relations among neighbours with special concern for those who may need special support; they raise money to cover their running expenses. Groups like these, without professional or full-time leadership, are glad to be able to call on the services of a community development worker. Help is given by the worker on general points of information. He is sometimes called in when there are difficulties on the committee, or in the youth section, and he can often represent a different point of view because of his experience. He can put one group in touch with another so that they may learn from each other. If required, he can organize conferences and discussions, and encourage these groups to express a

65

consumer point of view on housing or other matters.

There are a tremendous number of informal groups meeting in public houses, at work, in people's homes, which play an important part in social life and can sometimes be more helpful in tackling local problems than the official social agencies.

There are now detached workers in the youth service. It has been a great concern to many people that in spite of all that has been provided in clubs, evening classes, youth centres and youth organizations, the majority of young people do not make use of them. This would not matter if they had interests of their own which were stimulating and satisfying, but there is much evidence that this is not the case and that many young people have only superficial relationships with one another, and little contact with adults whom they can respect and like.

Since for various reasons many young people do not take advantage of the opportunities provided by the service of youth in the traditional setting of youth clubs, some workers try to make contact with them in a much less formal setting. They meet them in the streets and cafes. They get to know them and are sometimes able to work with small groups. The emphasis in this work is not on anything which is achieved in building up groups or introducing them to a wide range of activities, but in making some kind of relationship with individuals and helping them to relate to one another.

Changes are taking place in the youth clubs and centres. At one time there was a great deal of emphasis on loyalty to the club and its achievements. Local authorities often judge the success of a club by the number who attend it and the range and variety of their activities, those which have a strong cultural flavour often being rated above those of a social nature. Many youth leaders now see their clubs not so much in terms of interest groups as of friendship groups. It is in these small groups and in the inter-group relationships that young people are helped to their feet and grow and develop. Those people who work with groups should also be able to analyse what they are doing and why, and to be able to make a thoughtful assessment of what has been happening in relationships between various members of the group, and if necessary be able to write down his observations. The youth leader, by increasing his own self-awareness and understanding, can in this way be of more help to young people. This method of approach is sometimes referred to as social group work.

Community organization

There is another type of work in the community, which takes place at a different level. There are an immense number of voluntary organizations in every town and city, and there is always the danger of overlapping in their work or neglecting to meet some need which arises in the community which is not the special concern of any one of them. There is an important job to do in bringing together those agencies which are concerned in one or another with the welfare of the community, and discussing common problems. In towns there are councils of social service which perform just this function, and in the countryside rural community councils.

At present there is no special training for this type of community organization, although it requires administrative skill as well as a knowledge of the social services and of social policy, and some understanding of methods of research. Councils of social service can represent the view of the voluntary organizations to government or local government departments, and are available for consultation with them; they can discover needs in the community which are not being met, and decide what would be the best way of trying to meet them; they can experiment and make known the results of their experiments by publications and information services; they can arrange training for voluntary workers and direct them to the appropriate agencies. In some cases they have joint money-raising efforts, from which their constituent organizations benefit. As the social services, both voluntary and statutory, become more and more complicated, the need for this type of co-operation is the greater.

Co-operation in the field of youth work is achieved in different ways. Most affiliating bodies, such as the National Association of Youth Clubs and the National Federation of Boys' Clubs, provide a link between individual clubs, and offer training, the services of head-quarters officers, publications and other services to their members. There is also a Standing Conference of Voluntary Youth Organizations at the national level, and there are local conferences of this kind. On the statutory side there are county and county borough youth committees.

These youth committees could be very much more important than they sometimes are. In the complicated structure of the youth service, as it is at present, there is a need for youth committees, not only to recommend grant-aid and to discuss training and policy, but sometimes to initiate new work themselves. There should be sufficient staff for the youth officer, who is a servant of the local education authority, to be free to study in great detail the needs of the young people in his area.

Future trends

SOCIAL DEVELOPMENT IN NEW COMMUNITIES. Much of the present interest in community work has been stimulated by post-war housing programmes. It is slowly becoming recognized that with large movements of population to new towns, expanding towns, overspill estates, and redevelopment areas, there has to be social as well as physical planning if people are to enjoy their new environment. In the case of slum clearance, movement may be compulsory, and every effort has to be made to help people to adjust to the changes involved.

The new towns are a major experiment in housing. Built under the New Towns Act 1945, by development corporations set up by the Minister of Housing, they were unique in that industry was planned with the housing, and it was intended to provide all the amenities of a town. There were fifteen new towns started immediately after the war, and they have been successful enough for another group of new towns to be started. The planners have argued about density and design; the sociologists about age structure and class structure; and social workers about social amenities and ways in which people may be helped to settle down. The first new towns have provided considerable information about this type of social planning.

Out of this has emerged the concept of a new type of worker in the community – the social development officer. Not all the new towns have social development officers – in fact there are under half a dozen – and he is seldom called by that title, but may be known as a liaison officer, a public relations officer, or a social relations officer. The background of these men has been very different, and as yet there is no formal training for the job, nor even agreement on what it ought to be. Probably it is impossible to expect one man to fulfil all the functions which are necessary, and he needs to be in charge of a department in which other workers can supplement his skills.

In the first instance the social development officer needs to sit round the table with other chief officers at the planning stage. It is his job to see that the social implications of any aspect of the plan are fully considered. On some matters he may be able to give expert guidance, e.g. in the planning of community buildings and the use of open space.

While the timing and planning of the major social

services which are a statutory responsibility is a matter for the general manager of the corporation in co-operation with the local authorities concerned, the social development officer will want to know that there are adequate facilities for the many other services, both statutory and voluntary, which will be needed. It is particularly important that in the very early stages of development of each new housing area there are shops, public transport, a clinic, telephone box, etc. Some of these, like a communal meeting place or a shop, may have to be temporary, but it is essential to the well-being of the first families who move in that minimum facilities are provided, if not the full range.

It is arguable whether social research should be the responsibility of a social development officer. Somewhere on the corporation staff there must be a sociologist, advising on population structure, and finding out consumer opinion on many aspects of the development, and forecasting future needs. Many people think that this should be the responsibility of the social development department, possibly in co-operation with the Housing Manager.

Information is of vital importance to newcomers, who want to know how to get in touch with the various social services, what amenities the town provides and what its future development will be. Since people need help about personal problems such as hire-purchase a Citizens Advice Bureau to supplement the Corporation Information Centre is very desirable.

The social development officer is also concerned with what has previously been described as community development – with being available to any group or organization needing co-operation and help from outside. It may be the gardeners who want a place to store fertilizer, or a community association which is struggling into being and feels it ought to have a building;

or there may be the problem of a football team that has nowhere to play.

Whether one person is responsible for these different functions is not important. What really matters is that all of them are carried out. If this is necessary in a new town, why not in other housing areas? One Expanding Town has appointed special officers, but this is not generally done, and the need in large overspill estates is often very great. Community work of this specialized kind requires considerable ability. If such appointments were made, this would not remove from administrators all responsibility for the social aspects of the plan, but would supplement what they are doing. Only by understanding the human implications of physical and economic planning can the ultimate success of any plan be assured. Regional planning, like the planning of one small housing area, is planning for people. Technical experts might find it useful to have more sociologists and social development officers working as members of their team.

SOCIAL DEVELOPMENT IN DEPRESSED AREAS. Community work is of vital importance in new areas, but no less so in old-established districts where there are poor housing conditions and a multiplicity of social problems. Too little is known about the rehabilitation of such areas. It is in new areas that there is likely to be spontaneous community activity, and people will show initiative in solving their own problems. Community associations and tenants' associations, for example, will take action to look after their members. This is often not so in a depressed area. In spite of many old-established social agencies and good statutory social services, and perhaps the work of a local settlement, there is often an inability to reach down into the community in such a way that a significant change is brought about. Such a neighbourhood needs additional community workers.

The social workers

These workers can operate at two levels. First they need skill and time to work with the social agencies, discussing their problems, which are often considerable, and making it easier for them to work together. This may mean finding more money. At another level the worker may spend his time with informal groups and identify more immediately with the local people. Any action initiated by the people themselves to improve conditions is of great importance and should be assisted. Sometimes initiative on the part of local street groups or immigrants needs interpretation to administrators and established organizations.

At present it is rare to have workers in the community with the freedom to undertake work at either of these levels because of lack of staff, money and sometimes vision in the voluntary organizations, and lack of flexibility in statutory ones. There are difficult areas, however, where this is starting to happen.

Training for community work

It is a relatively new idea in this country that social workers should train to work with groups and communities as well as with individuals and the family. In casework there is well-defined employment, and students know what is expected of them if they want to be medical, psychiatric or family welfare workers, or to be probation or child care officers.

In groups and community work employment is still ill defined, and training for it hard to come by. Pioneer work has been done by the Tavistock Institute of Human Relations, Nuffield College Oxford, and in the Community Development course at the Institute of Education, London. In general, however, practice in the field is probably ahead of theory in the university.

Universities vary in the courses they offer. It may be a one-year professional training, or a few sessions in some aspect of community work given by a visiting lecturer. Training may be located in the department concerned with education or social studies or administration. It may be called group work, community development or community organization, and to add to the confusion, different people use these words to mean different things. There is now a two-year full time training course for community centre wardens, with a certificate awarded by the Institute of Education, Birmingham, and a one-year training course for youth leaders at a special college in Leicestershire.

The future of community work

Community work is likely in the future to be one of the most important branches of social work. It is not, however, confined to a few people who are said to be doing 'community work'. Those with a professional role to play will all benefit, whether they are case workers, teachers, youth leaders, health visitors, doctors, clergy, housing managers or administrators, from some understanding of community work. In the same way the community worker can gain from their special knowledge. It should be only a matter of time before training is available to community workers in the way it is now available to case workers. Since both have the same basis in human relations the time may come when they will train together.

The disabled and the handicapped

JOHN H. NICHOLSON

Dr Nicholson has been involved in social work since 1913, when he went to live in a University settlement after leaving Oxford. In 1956 he was invited by the National Council of Social Service to make a survey of provisions for the handicapped and disabled, for a joint committee of the Council and of the Carnegie United Kingdom Trust. This report was published in 1958, under the title of *Help for the handicapped*. He later served as a member of a committee formed to investigate the problems of the handicapped school leaver, and is now Chairman of a working party for the National Society for Mentally Handicapped Children. Formerly Vice-Chancellor of the University of Hull, he is also a Vice-President of the Association of Social Workers.

Who are the handicapped?

As the word is used in the social services, a handicap is a permanent disability – one that cannot be put right. A man with a broken leg is, of course, out of action for the time being. But he is not technically 'handicapped', unless he is left with some permanent loss of function. Handicaps range from complete crippling to some slight mutilation (such as the loss of a finger) or loss of normal movement (for instance, inability to raise an arm beyond a certain point). They may arise from some failure in pre-natal development (the 'thalidomide babies' are an obvious example), from disease (for instance, polio-myelitis), or from accident. They may be stable (usually the case where accident is the cause) or progressive (as in muscular dystrophy). This chapter is concerned only with physical handicap; mental handicaps are dealt with elsewhere.

How much a handicap matters depends not only on its

severity but on how much it interferes with what one would otherwise be capable of doing. Those born handicapped, once they have learned to live as full a life as their limitations allow, have no further adjustment to make. The blind from birth are an outstanding example of what can be achieved. Those whose handicap is the result of accident or disease may have to change not only their occupation but their whole way of life. When surgical and medical skills and, perhaps, physiotherapy have done what is possible to minimize the damage, the remaining disability must be accepted. This is never easy; it is hard to accept that one has climed one's last mountain, played one's last game of football, must no longer drive a car, must sleep downstairs or live between a bed and a wheelchair; harder still to abandon the hope of resuming some skilled occupation, perhaps even of ever again earning one's living. In all this, stable handicaps are easier to accept and adjust to than the ups and downs characteristic of some crippling diseases (for instance, multiple sclerosis) or the epileptic fits which may lead to losing a job for which, during ninety-nine per cent of the time, one is fully competent. Hardest of all to accept are deteriorating conditions which, in the earlier stages, interfere little if at all with normal functioning – Parkinson's disease is an obvious example.

The needs of the handicapped

What handicapped people most *desire* is to be restored to what they regard as normal life, and the aim of rehabilitation is to help to do this wherever possible. A skilled fitter, working at the bench, who has lost the use of his legs, is still as good as the next man as a worker, though he needs special transport to his place of work. In other cases, the disability deprives them of some function essential to their work: they can no longer lift, or stand, or work where there is dust, or operate powered machinery, or their sight is impaired. In many such cases, given training for a different type of work, they can return to industry as skilled craftsmen or in another capacity.

Some, while capable of being trained for productive work, can no longer stand the pace, or the physical conditions, of an ordinary workshop. They are, however, able to work at their trade under 'sheltered' conditions, in a shop designed and organized to meet their needs. In either case, these people keep, or regain, their standing as wage-earners; this is important, not only because they need to earn but to their self-esteem and to their status in the family. There are also home-working projects, but these have not, up to now, been very successful, except in the case of the blind, where well-organized schemes are supported by a body of highly trained teachers.

Those for whom employment is no longer possible still need occupation, preferably in the company of other men and women. Centres where they could do various kinds of craft-work have been organized for many years past by voluntary bodies. This has now been largely replaced by 'sub-contract' work on simple processes for industrial firms. Wages are not paid, but small sums can be earned without incurring a deduction from any grant they may be receiving from public funds. In the last few years, many such centres have been opened by local authorities, and they are now an established part of the provision made for handicapped people. Those whose handicap does not allow them to take part even in such activities as these may be helped to practice some 'pastimes' in their own homes.

Accident or disease may also cripple a housewife. She can, if needs be, learn to keep house from a wheel chair, provided that some necessary adaptations to the house are made. There must be no stairs to climb, and doors must be made wide enough to let the chair pass, and be easily opened. Everything she needs to use must be within her reach, sitting in the chair: stove, sink, taps, cupboards and shelves. If her hands are crippled, there are ingenious 'aids' for turning taps and to help in carrying out various household chores. The bedroom, bathroom and toilet must also be suitably adapted.

It is important that disabled people, especially those who are otherwise competent, should be enabled to move around, in the house and outside, as freely as their condition allows. Great progress has been made in recent years in fitting artificial limbs, but for disabled people who have not the free use of their legs, natural or artificial, some form of transport is a basic need. Hand-propelled wheel chairs provide this inside the house and for short distances outside. For longer journeys, there are powered chairs known as 'tricycles', and cars with adapted controls for those who can obtain and drive them.

For most men, and for an increasing number of women, to live at home, in lodgings, or perhaps in a hostel and go out to work is a 'normal' life. This can be possible for many young handicapped workers if specially designed homes are provided for them – otherwise they may have to stay in hospital and be denied the opportunity to work. Gravely disabled people who need continuous medical or nursing care must, anyhow, remain in hospital.

Housing, employment and transport are basic needs but if handicapped people are to live as full a life as their disability allows, they also need a variety of what are called welfare services. These include opportunities to meet together and to share in the social life of the general community; to go on holiday; to share, if they wish, in the 'games' now organized for handicapped people; and to be supplied with whatever personal aids they need to enable them to take part. They may also need the professional services of physiotherapists, occupational therapists and chiropodists, home help and 'meals on wheels', and personal service for all kinds of everyday chores which the able-bodied take in their stride – shopping, changing library books, taking messages and the like.

Policy has changed radically during the last few years. The aim is now to do everything possible to enable handicapped people to live in the community, rather than in 'institutions' of any kind. This calls for the provision of whatever services are necessary in their own homes (known as 'domiciliary services') or, where that is impracticable, in specially built or adapted accommodation in a community setting. The social worker's function is to establish and maintain the necessary contacts, to help handicapped people in finding a solution to their personal difficulties, and in general, to give support in whatever ways are most likely to increase, rather than diminish, their capacity to accept responsibility for the conduct of their own lives.

Who provides services?

Voluntary societies were the pioneers in providing for the handicapped. Services for the blind and the deaf have long been highly organized. A large number of charitable foundations were established in the last century to provide for those needing residential care. Some of these catered for particular groups; others were open without distinction to those needing such care, including the handicapped; some were specifically for 'cripples'. There were also a large number of 'cripples' clubs', which generally accepted as members anyone suffering from a marked degree of deformity or physical disfunction, however caused, but not in general, those otherwise disabled by disease. They organized social activities and generally taught handicrafts. Workshops for the blind were among the earliest schemes for the training and employment of handicapped people. Other voluntary bodies provided particular services for individuals, especially for children: for example, holiday camps.

Before the Second World War, the blind were the only group of adult handicapped people recognized by law, though there were already special schools for handicapped children.

Responsibility for public provision was established by the Disabled Persons (Employment) Act, 1944, and the National Assistance Act, 1948. Broadly speaking, the Ministry of Labour is responsible for matters relating to employment, while social welfare is the responsibility of the local authorities acting through their health and welfare committees, under the general direction of the Ministry of Health. Disablement is defined in the widest terms: it includes not only injury and congenital deformity but the effects of disease.[1] For administrative and statistical purposes, the blind and the deaf are included among the physically handicapped.[2]

It might be thought that, with the entry of the state into the field, the voluntary bodies would wither away. On the contrary, with few exceptions, their work has not only continued, but developed. There were several reasons for this. Local authorities were, for the most part, slow to start schemes. While recurrent economic crises delayed building projects, the new policy of keeping the handicapped in the community called for extensive domiciliary services, and there was (and still is) an acute shortage of qualified staff, including social workers. Local authorities were asked to submit to the Ministry of Health staged development plans, covering the period up to 1972, and these were later revised after consultation with the Ministry.[3] Meanwhile, it came to be recognized that partnership between local authorities

[1] *Disabled Persons (Employment) Act, 1944.*

[2] Ministry of Health *Health and welfare: the development of community care* H.M.S.O., 1963. Cmnd. 1973, p. 30.

[3] Ministry of Health *Health and welfare: the development of community care. Revision to 1973–1974* H.M.S.O., 1964.

and voluntary bodies in this field was not merely a stopgap measure. The Ministry issued a series of circulars to local authorities urging them to consult and co-operate with voluntary bodies.

In a number of areas, these bodies established Associations for the Physically Handicapped on a county basis – a movement stimulated by the Central Council for the Care of Cripples (now the Central Council for the Disabled). Many new voluntary bodies were formed, most of them to promote the welfare of particular groups: those suffering from cerebral palsy ('spastics'), epilepsy, multiple sclerosis, muscular dystrophy or haemophilia are examples. In most cases, the initiative was taken by parents.

Assessment, rehabilitation, education and training

Rehabilitation starts in hospital, but it does not end when the patient is discharged. It should follow him out into the community and see him well settled back at home, and if possible, in his old job or some other if he cannot now cope with that. Recovering from a serious illness or injury is, at best, a tedious business. If there is added anxiety of an uncertain future, perhaps with the knowledge that he can never fully recover the use of arms or legs or live as he used to do, the prospect seems grim. He will be introduced to whatever 'aids' he may need, and taught to use them.

There will be occupational therapy and perhaps a workshop where he can try out his skill and recover muscle tone. A disabled housewife may find in the hospital an adapted kitchen, or even possibly a whole house in miniature, where she can learn new ways of doing familiar tasks. But if the disabled are to co-operate fully, they need reassurance and support as well as skilled treatment and help. Rehabilitation is a team job, calling for many different skills, all directed to solving the problems of the patient as an individual. The British

Medical Association has estimated that 25 per cent of orthopaedic, 10 per cent of medical, and a small percentage of surgical cases need rehabilitation in this sense.[1]

The hospital team needs to be in touch with the team that will – or should – take over when the patient leaves. Some hospitals hold, shortly before discharge, case-conferences which those who will be responsible for his welfare in the community are invited to attend, including the Disablement Resettlement Officer. With the growth of community services, this seems essential if there is not to be a break in care just when continuity is most needed. The 'day centres' now established by some hospitals for the mentally ill provide a valuable link between hospital and community. King's College Hospital was among the pioneers in establishing, years ago, a centre of this kind for some orthopaedic cases. Others, after discharge, need further rehabilitation, related directly to employment or to training for industry.

Two voluntary colleges, Queen Elizabeth's at Leatherhead and St Loyes at Exeter, were the pioneers in the industrial rehabilitation and training of the disabled. Their founders accepted, and used to the full, handicapped people's longing for normality. They stressed that handicaps are *specific* – those who suffer from them are 'disabled' only for the particular activities which their handicap prevents them from carrying out. Two further colleges, the Finchale Training Centre, County Durham, and the Portland Training College, near Mansfield, Nottinghamshire, were founded later. The colleges, and those training there, are assisted by government grants. The percentage of successes is remarkable, in spite of the severity of many handicaps. A visitor to one of these colleges was received at the lodge by an attractive girl in her twenties, strapped to a sloping board, but operating

[1] Evidence submitted by the British Medical Association to the Interdepartmental Committee on Rehabilitation and Resettlement, 1954.

her telephones with nimble fingers – a perfect example of how 'specific' even a serious handicap can be.

It was not until 1944 that the Disabled Persons (Employment) Act established services for the handicapped under the Ministry of Labour. There are now seventeen Industrial Rehabilitation Units in different parts of the country and just under 134,000 people have completed the courses provided there.[1] The I.R.U.'s do not train for particular trades. Their purpose is to assess the capacity of those who attend and help them to recover basic skills and 'tone up'. Those who then need a trade training may go on to a Government Training Centre, where they will work side by side with others not handicapped, or if they are too severely disabled, to one of the voluntary training colleges, which receive financial support from the Ministry. Training may also be given at a technical or commercial college or with an employer. The D.R.O.'s keep a register of disabled persons suitable for employment in open industry or under sheltered conditions. They may recommend admission to an Industrial Rehabilitation Unit or other rehabilitation or training course. The Government Training Centres offer, between them, some forty courses in skilled trades, mostly for industrial, but also for clerical occupations, hairdressing (which seems specially favoured by handicapped men), repairing typewriters, watches or clocks, radio and television sets.

The work of St Dunstan's is well known; it has created a new public image for the blind. In the workshops for the blind, training for the traditional crafts of brushmaking and the like is rapidly giving place to training in industrial processes, using powered machinery. At the Homes of Recovery for the newly blinded, at Torquay, they are taught, among other skills, pottery and various crafts, though not as a vocational training. There is also fitting and drilling, using a micrometer

[1] *Ministry of Labour Gazette* March, 1965, p. 117.

with braille numerals. At the centre established at Hethersett by the Royal National Institute for the Blind, young people are given, in addition to further education, 'pre-vocational training in manual dexterity – light engineering, light crafts, telephony, typewriting, etc.[1]

Progress in techniques is transforming the services for the deaf. Electronics, for example, has made hearing possible for many who were otherwise below the threshold of audible sound. Early and accurate ascertainment is now possible, and is vital as the following case illustrates.

Marie is an illegitimate girl. Her mother – of whom nothing is known – placed her with a foster mother soon after she was born, and she was 'taken into care' by the Children's Department. At two years old she was not able to sit up and was not talking, and she was late at all her 'milestones'. She also had weakness on her left side. Her foster mother felt unable to give her the attention she needed, and the Children's Officer arranged for her to go into a hospital for retarded children. There she was found to be very severely deaf. After appropriate treatment, she began slowly to make progress and she is now, at the age of seven, being given a trial in a small Roman Catholic school for physically handicapped children.

There has been similar progress in other fields. Many forms of epilepsy can now be completely controlled by drugs, or the frequency and severity of the fits greatly reduced. The Spastics Society includes among some twenty residential centres, five boarding schools for sufferers from cerebral palsy, an assessment centre at Hawksworth Hall, Guiseley, Leeds and a training centre at Sherrards, Welwyn. There are also about 100 day centres.[2] Like other voluntary societies for the handicapped, the aim is to provide, for those capable of it, a

[1] British Council for the Rehabilitation of the Disabled *The handicapped school leaver* The Council, 1964. p. 53 quotes Ministry of Labour *Services for the disabled* H.M.S.O., 2nd edn. 1961, p. 56.
[2] The Spastics Society *Annual report, 1964.*

training which will lead to employment either in open industry or in sheltered workshops, and for the rest, whatever opportunities they need to live as full a life as their handicap, in each case, allows.

In January 1962 there were 15,583 children in special schools for the physically handicapped, including epileptics, the deaf and those with partial hearing, and the blind and those with partial sight.[1] There were 124 day schools and 109 boarding schools. Of the day schools, 122 were maintained by local authorities, only 2, both for physically handicapped children, were provided by voluntary bodies. On the other hand, voluntary bodies provided 63 of the boarding schools, of which 26 were for the physically handicapped. In the opinion of a working party of the British Council for the Rehabilitation of the Disabled, which reported in 1964, the provision of schools for the *physically* handicapped, 'existing or contemplated, would appear to meet the needs as at present ascertained'.[2]

Employment

In administrative terms, 'employment' means 'work for pay or gain', as distinct from maintenance, which is assessed, not on worth, but on need. Disabled people may be employed either in 'open' industry or in sheltered workshops. Those who attend day centres where occupational work is provided, may earn small sums, but they are not regarded as employed. Registration as a disabled person (other than the blind) is voluntary, but the Ministry of Labour, through the D.R.O., must be satisfied that those who apply are fit for employment. In April, 1964, out of a working population of about 25 million, 655,878 were registered as disabled. In February, 1965, some 50,000 of those on the register were unemployed;

---

[1] Memorandum by the Ministry of Education in *The handicapped school leaver*, Appendix 4. *op. cit.*

[2] *The handicapped school leaver*, p. 30. *op. cit.*

of these about 44,000 were suitable for ordinary employment, the rest for employment under sheltered conditions.[1]

The first priority for disabled workers is open industry,
where the great majority are, in fact, employed. While
employers with substantial numbers of workers must
now, by law, employ 3 per cent of disabled men and
women, and some are no doubt only slightly handicapped, the claim that the disabled hold their place in
industry on their merits is well founded. They now
include many blind workers.

In sheltered employment, as in the training colleges,
voluntary bodies were the pioneers. There are now over
thirty such workshops; they receive deficiency grants
from the Ministry of Labour, provided that they con-
form to normal industrial conditions and wages, and
that the work done is of real economic value. Their
products include woodwork, basketry, bookbinding,
boot-repairing, surgical boots and appliances, electric
blankets, machine knitting, toy making and such women's
crafts as the hand-printed fabrics made at the Yateley
Industries for Disabled Girls, Hampshire, and the fine
needlework of the School of Stitchery and Lace at Great
Bookham, Surrey.

Remploy, an autonomous company set up under the
Disabled Persons (Employment) Act, 1944, has eighty-
eight sheltered workshops, employing nearly 7,000
people. It is a commercial concern, with ordinary trading
and productive activities, but subsidized from government funds. The voluntary training colleges already
described employ in their workshops severely disabled
men and women who are not suited to open industry. In
recent years, there has been a marked increase in the
number of sheltered workshops provided by local
authorities under the National Assistance Act, 1948. The

[1] *Ministry of Labour Gazette*, March, 1965, p. 134.

Ministry of Labour is now responsible for approving their schemes for sheltered employment and makes grants towards the cost.

Most of those who find their way back to industry through industrial rehabilitation are skilled workers who have met with a crippling accident or illness. By no means all of them must go on from an Industrial Rehabilitation Unit to a Government Training Centre, nor have the majority of those attending Government Training Centres passed through an Industrial Rehabilitation Unit.

Only a minority of those employed by Remploy have been to either. Remploy may, indeed, be the first experience of disciplined work. An epileptic in his thirties, whose fits had been largely controlled, was accepted, without having previously worked in industry. When he was seen at the bench, after nine months, he had had no fit since he was taken on – and he had married. But the best chance of success is to start training young. Most young disabled entrants to industry have been handicapped from birth, though some – early victims of poliomyelitis, or those injured in childhood or early adolescence – have acquired handicaps. In either case, they need special help in training and in seeking employment. The Ministry of Labour appoints Youth Employment Officers who advise special school leavers and help them to find employment; local authorities had the option to appoint such officers and a few have done so.

A working party appointed by the British Council for Rehabilitation to investigate the needs of handicapped school leavers reported in 1964. This Report, while paying tribute to the work of the D.R.O.'s and Youth Employment Officers, questioned the finding of a pilot survey conducted by the Ministry of Labour that 94 per cent of handicapped school leavers had obtained a satisfactory start in employment,[1] and suggested a lower figure of 85 per cent successes.

A government committee under the Chairmanship of Lord Piercy,[2] reporting in 1956, had urged closer co-operation between officers of statutory and voluntary bodies concerned with the training and employment of the disabled. Nearly ten years later, the British Council for Rehabilitation Committee stressed that better co-ordination between all the services responsible (including the special schools) was still one of the most urgent needs. In particular, they regretted the break at the school leaving age, when the responsibility of the school health service ends, and they recommended extension to 18.[3] The Youth Employment Officer and the D.R.O. should work more closely together. Assessment should be a continuous process and satisfactory settlement in employment should not be assumed until after a longer period.

Social welfare

The present policy of keeping the handicapped in the community whenever, and as long as, possible, makes big demands on both the statutory and the voluntary bodies providing community services. County councils and county borough councils are responsible for the public welfare services. These include, for the physically handicapped, residential Homes and Day Centres, and the so-called 'domiciliary services' – health visitors, home helps, home nurses and social workers – which the handicapped share with others needing them.

In March, 1964, there were in England and Wales

---

[1] *The handicapped school leaver* pp. 14–15 and Appendix 3, *op. cit.*

[2] Ministry of Labour *Report of the Committee of Enquiry on the rehabilitation, training and resettlement of disabled persons* H.M.S.O., 1956. Cmnd. 9883.

[3] *The handicapped school leaver:* Recommendation I. *op. cit.*

1,328 day centres for the physically handicapped, provided by local authorities. In December 1964, the authorities employed on welfare 5,830 health visitors, 29,338 home helps, 8,137 home nurses, and 3,277 social workers.[1] The main services now provided by one large county borough are described below. The growth of these services has now been planned by all local authorities responsible over the next ten years. The main difficulty in realizing these plans is the acute shortage of qualified staff.

How many physically handicapped people are there, and how many of them use the local authorities' services? It is impossible to say. Local authorities keep a register, but apart in 1963 from the blind (96,474), the partially sighted (27,020), the deaf (24,496) and the hard of hearing (16,981), the number of the so-called general classes, (which include all the rest) was registered as 121,369;[2] surely a mere fraction of those eligible. The explanation seems to be that since registration is voluntary, only those register who need to use the services. While, in that case, registration confers advantages, it may be felt to mark a man and prejudice his chances in other ways.

The National Assistance Act, 1948, defines the powers of local authorities in the field of welfare. Voluntary bodies are not bound by such definitions, or by regulations which, however flexible, set limits to what they are permitted to do.

For them, welfare may, and often does, include services within the scope of government departments other than the Ministry of Health. While the social services of the welfare state now provide for all general needs, there are still special needs and emergencies to be

[1] *Health and welfare: the development of community care. Revision to 1973 – 1974* H.M.S.O., 1964, pp. 324–5, *op. cit.*
[2] Ministry of Health *Report for 1963* H.M.S.O., 1964. Cmnd. 2389. Table 50, p. 118.

met. There are, then, still cases where grants or gifts to individuals from voluntary sources are called for. But their main contribution to welfare is personal service.

The less mobile handicapped need, besides housing, food and perhaps skilled treatment, some opportunity for social life and occupation. The 'cripples' clubs' (now mostly called Clubs for the Physically Handicapped), with their tea, talk and handicrafts were formed to supply this. Fostered by the Central Council for the Disabled, county associations for the welfare of the physically handicapped were organized and affiliated to the Central Council. Advice and help on every aspect of disablement was made available to them, and conferences provided an opportunity for pooling experience.

The *Handbook and directory of voluntary social services*[1] lists some forty voluntary bodies concerned with the handicapped, in most cases the physically handicapped. These are, in the main, national bodies. They provide advice and guidance and seek to educate the public in the nature and problems of a particular disability, and some of them foster research. Seventeen of these bodies have local branches or organize locally such activities as clubs or centres.

There may, then, in any one town be a number of separate activities for the handicapped, most of them serving those suffering from a particular disability, but also one or more clubs or centres, provided by the local authority or organized by a voluntary body, admitting anyone who is physically handicapped.

Voluntary bodies and individual volunteers give service in too many ways to be separately described, and impossible to classify; they can only be illustrated. They provide transport in private cars, organize holidays and camps for children. They offer particular services, such as the w.v.s. 'meals on wheels'. They 'stand in' to

---

[1] National Council of Social Service, 1964 (revised).

The social workers

fill a gap in the established services, as the British Red Cross Society has often done. Their advisory services, such as the Citizens' Advice Bureau and the Marriage Guidance Council, are available to the handicapped as to others. They can often relieve hard-pressed professional workers of chores which are necessary, but time-consuming.

There is no overall pattern; schemes vary from area to area. There is clearly a danger of overlapping, or even a conflict of view or interest, between statutory and voluntary bodies and between voluntary bodies themselves. But, given a friendly and co-operative attitude on both sides, a fruitful partnership results.

Residential care

The growth of community services has not diminished the need for residential care, but its character has changed. The welfare state inherited from the old poor law large buildings – formerly workhouses – which were the last refuge of so many handicapped people. As for the old, the policy is now to replace this type of accommodation by Homes of moderate size, adapted to their needs. In 1964 local authorities provided 69 such homes, housing 6,331 people. There were also 3,749 places available for the disabled in Homes for people aged 65 and over, and 2,582 Homes for those under 65. The ten year plan proposes 118 Homes for the physically handicapped by 1974.[1]

In this field again, individual benefactors and voluntary bodies were the pioneers. The local authority now has the duty to inspect and register voluntary Homes. In 1963 there were 164 such Homes for disabled people with 5,955 places and a further 277 Homes with 5,484 places for 'old persons and disabled persons'.

In that year, local authorities placed 1,155 elderly and

[1] *Health and welfare: the development of community care. Revision to 1973 – 1974* H.M.S.O., 1964, p. 324, *op. cit.*

90

physically handicapped people, and 1,719 younger disabled, in these Homes, by arrangement with the voluntary bodies concerned.[1] The voluntary Homes are much less standardized than those of the local authorities. Broadly speaking, they take more severely handicapped people. They serve a variety of purposes. Some, like the most recent addition to this field, the Cheshire Homes, provide permanent care for those for whom neither the hospital nor an ordinary Home is appropriate. Others, e.g. those established by the Spastics Society, combine residence with treatment. Some provide for disabled ex-Service men: the Star and Garter Home, Richmond, Surrey, is a well-known example. There is a group which have sheltered workshops attached. Examples are 'Sherrards'; the Spastic Society's Training Centre at Welwyn; the Searchlight Cripples Workshop at Newhaven for severely disabled boys; St George's House, Harrogate, which takes both those severely handicapped of high intelligence, and others with a slight handicap of low intelligence; John Groom's Crippleage at Mill Hill, where girls make artificial flowers; and the Homes for disabled girls at Yately and Great Bookham.

Disabled people who are still capable of work may be unemployed if the journey to work is too far or too difficult for them. The solution is to provide residence, with whatever special facilities they need, within the distance they can travel. An outstanding example is Duchess of Gloucester House, Isleworth, which houses paraplegic men who work at skilled trades in neighbouring factories. Following a pioneer scheme of the Norwich local authority, some other authorities are now establishing Homes where disabled young men, capable of travelling short distances to work, can be housed.

Among special needs, provision for some of the most

[1] Ministry of Health *Report for 1963* H.M.S.O., 1964. Cmnd. 2389, pp. 114–15, *op. cit.*

difficult cases is urgent. Muscular dystrophy and double incontinence are examples. Special difficulty also arises in cases of multiple handicaps. The Shaftesbury Society, among others, has converted accommodation not now needed for its original purpose to take such cases.

What a local authority provides

An overall picture of what an active local authority is now doing for the handicapped can best be seen by taking an example. Kingston-upon-Hull, Yorkshire, has a population of just over 300,000. Services for the disabled are administered by three Departments – Education, Health, and Welfare. The general social services are also available to the physically handicapped, as to others who need their help. Staff employed in the domiciliary services in 1964 included 29 social workers, 41 health visitors, 46 home nurses and 258 home helps.[1]

There are four special schools for physically handicapped children. Two of these have an age-range of 3 to 16. One of these, with 105 places, includes cerebral palsy among the physical handicaps provided for. It has a medical unit and a hydrotherapy bath. The second, with 60 places, is for the deaf and partially deaf. Loop hearing and other special aids are provided, and lip reading and speech communication are taught. The staff share the work at the audiology unit and assist in assessment. A third school, for the partially sighted, with an age-range of 5 to 16, has a special curriculum. A feature of this building is the use, in classroom decoration, of colours easily distinguished. The fourth school, for delicate children, includes those with heart trouble. It has 210 places and an age-range of 7 to 16. Special buses, and taxis, take children to and from school. There is also teaching at home and in hospital. Where boarding school education is recommended, this is arranged.

[1] *Health and welfare: the development of community care. Revision to 1973 – 1974* H.M.S.O., 1964, p. 39, *op. cit.*

92

The disabled and the handicapped

There is a supplementary course for teachers of handicapped children in the authority's College of Education.

Two services provided by the Health Department call for special mention. Selected health visitors have been specially trained to detect deafness in children at the age of six months. Where this is suspected, an audiometric test is arranged, and the advice of a consultant is available. Three occupational therapists who visit the homes of handicapped people are included in the establishment of the Department. The 'diversionary work' they teach ranges from simple handicrafts to small-scale printing. The authority has a small shop where the products are sold. They also give training for a change of work where this is advised.

The Welfare Department at Hull has a comprehensive scheme of services.[1] Most of these are of the types already described; a few figures will best illustrate their scope. But there are also special features. Some 939 blind and partially blind are registered, and provided with the usual follow-up and employment services. Training and sheltered employment are available locally, and there is a hostel for blind workers. Special transport to a day centre and to social and recreational activities is available. There are 404 people registered as deaf with speech, deaf without speech or hard of hearing.

Specialized services are available for each of these three groups, and there is a day centre for them.

The 'general classes' registered number 2,426. The services include three day centres where meals, occupation and entertainment are provided, coaches with tail lifts for those in chairs and other personal aids they need. Sheltered employment is available in the workshops for the blind. Grants can be made towards the cost of annual holidays. There is a home visiting service, and handicrafts are taught by seven full-time and thirty

[1] Kingston-upon-Hull Welfare Services Committee *Annual report of the Director of Welfare Services for 1964.*

part-time instructors. In 1964, 208 adaptations to property were made or special aids installed there. The authority has nineteen small Homes for 'elderly persons and others' and the physically handicapped can, in suitable cases, be housed there. Disabled people can also be placed in some of the fifteen voluntary Homes – three in Hull – where the committee has made special arrangements. Work has started on a purpose-built Home for the younger disabled.

How far are the needs met?

There is no overall assessment of the total need, and no reliable estimate is available except for such groups as the blind and the deaf. The registers of the school medical officers, the Ministry of Labour and the local welfare authorities serve different purposes and are based on different standards of disability. The extent to which known needs are met varies widely from area to area, as the tables in the Ministry of Health's reports show. Among the most urgent needs are residential care for the severely handicapped who do not require constant medical treatment, for those suffering from multiple handicaps or from deteriorating diseases, and for the doubly incontinent; and many more hostels to house young handicapped workers. However what can be said is that, for the physically handicapped as a whole, things are moving after a slow start.

Problems of old age

ANTHONY M. REES

This essay on the problems of old people surveys one of the largest areas of social welfare, in which the voluntary and statutory agencies have to work particularly close together. Work ranging from pre-retirement courses to care of the elderly sick extends over a broad section of the population.

Anthony Rees is a sociologist, who, after leaving Cambridge, worked for the Acton Society Trust in London, where he worked on a number of projects, including a study of local councillors in East London. He later worked on a Bristol University survey on the impact of large scale industrial installations in country areas. Since 1962 he has been Senior Research Assistant in the Department of Social Theory and Institutions at Durham University, where he has been studying the social service provided for the elderly in a local country borough, under a Rowntree Trust Grant.

In 1951 109 people in every 1,000 of the population were aged 65 or over; by 1961 the proportion had risen to 118; and in 1982, if the Registrar General's estimates prove correct, it will be 137. These figures have been viewed with concern by some commentators, partly because of the growing unfavourableness of the ratio between the working and dependent populations which they reflect; and partly because of the fear that in an age where the small nuclear family has become the norm, old people will no longer be able to rely on the support from relatives which sustained them in the past. This ties in with a popular stereotype, which sees the typical old age pensioner as frail, poor and probably neglected by children and neighbours.

Perspective

In these circumstances it is important to keep a sense of

perspective, and to define the 'problems of old age' more closely. Research has repeatedly shown that old people as a group make substantial demands on the social services. But bare figures of proportions and trends tell us little without careful interpretation. The elderly do not constitute a homogeneous section of the community. The years from retirement to death may represent a quarter of a lifetime, and it is obvious nonsense to say that a hale and hearty sixty-five year old (or even more a woman who has just passed sixty if minimum pensionable age is taken as the criterion) presents the same problems as a frail and housebound person of eighty-five. Even chronological age is not necessarily a good guide to health and capacity: individual differences between those of the same age may substantially outweigh the differences between the ages.

The extent of the problem also differs markedly from place to place. For example the less prosperous areas of the country, like Scotland and the North East have a notably young population, and are not, as the popular view has it, burdened with a greater than average proportion of the elderly because of migration by the younger people to the honeyed lands of the South. Geographically there are also significant differences in the proportions of old people living alone. Overall, a comparative international survey found that 22 per cent of respondents were living alone, a figure not very dissimilar to that found in other industrialized countries (Denmark 27.7 per cent, United States 21.5 per cent). Cole and Utting found that 17 to 18 per cent of those interviewed in such diverse areas as Hexham Rural District and Glasgow were 'keeping house alone in unshared accommodation'; while in Leicester the proportion was 37 per cent. 'Living alone' is not synonymous with 'social isolation', as determined by frequency of contact with others. Nevertheless, there is a positive relationship between the two. Tunstall found that 68 per cent of the old people living alone[1] in his sample were socially isolated[2] (having fewer than 20 to 21 contacts a week) compared with 21 per cent of all old people. Clearly all these factors may affect the demands for social service.

There is one further factor which makes the intervention of the social services at some point more likely – childlessness – and this is probably the most important of them all. In Townsend's survey of 304 in-patients in an East London geriatric hospital in 1955, 15 per cent of the married or widowed men and 33 per cent of the women possessed no surviving children – compared with 10 per cent and 9 per cent respectively in the general sample. The figures for those admitted to residential accommodation proved the point even more strongly. Altogether, around 30 per cent of the elderly have no surviving offspring, and they, not those with families, make the major demands.

Two or three children probably constitute the best possible investment for old age. There is no evidence at all of mass neglect of old people by their offspring: quite the contrary in fact. About half of those with surviving children are actually living in the same dwelling as a son or daughter, and a high percentage of the rest have at least one married child within five minutes walk.[3] Frequent contact is the rule rather than the exception. Tunstall showed that only 7 per cent of those with living children had no contact with them (or with their spouses) during the month prior to interview, while 64 per cent of them had five or more contacts in the previous week. The assistance given by children, and especially by daughters, goes far beyond an occasional friendly chat.

[1] Jeremy Tunstall *Old and alone* (as yet unpublished).
[2] Peter Townsend *The family life of old people* (Reports of Institute of Community Studies, 2.) Routledge, 1957.
[3] D. Cole and J. E. G. Utting *The economic circumstances of old people* Welwyn: Codicote, P., 1962.

In some instances, their sacrifices may be extreme. A country G.P., Dr Miller, gives a good example:[1] a married man, 'with wide commitments, who brought his aged mother from some distance to live with him in her extreme old age. She was in advanced and irrevocable senile dementia, almost completely paralysed as a result of two shattering strokes, totally blind, and doubly incontinent. He nursed her devotedly, feeding her, bathing her daily, changing the bedclothes when necessary, and even washing them himself. He refused all offers of help from his wife and family, and when it was suggested to him that a bed in a nearby hospital would be made available for her, he replied: "I am doing for her only what she did for me when I was helpless; she wouldn't let anyone else do it. Nor will I".' An exceptional case, certainly; but the picture it presents is considerably nearer the norm than the popular conception of old people being callously deserted by their offspring.

A survey in Lewisham illustrates very clearly the crucial importance of the family in sustaining its older members. Nearly 90 per cent of those having difficulty with housework; and 83 per cent of those having difficulty in getting their meals are helped by relatives. Thus the majority of old people continue to enjoy a full life, as members of an extended family. A striking feature is that class differences are not important. Roughly equal proportions of those men who were employed in middle-class occupations (or their spouses) and of those with a manual working-class background, live alone, or are socially isolated, or admit to sometimes or often feeling lonely. The belief that all working-class old people belong to a richer and more satisfying kinship network, and that middle-class children leave their elderly parents without adequate care, appears to be a myth.

---

[1] H. C. Miller *The ageing countryman* National Corporation for the Care of Old People, 1963.

The process of ageing

Ageing is a natural process, and a gradual one. As people grow older their horizon will tend to narrow and their expectations to lessen. They are often unaware that this has happened. Richardson, in a study in North-East Scotland, found that when old people were asked to rate their health, similar proportions of those of 70 years or over said that it was good or very good as did those of 60 to 69.[1] Objectively, this was not the case: a substantially higher proportion of the over-70's suffered from limited mobility. The old people, however, did not answer according to any objective criterion; they rated themselves according to what they thought was expected of them at their age.

In this way ageing involves a series of slow and generally harmonious withdrawals. At the same time it focuses attention on the shocks or 'discontinuities' to which a minority find extreme difficulty in adapting. Retirement may be one such sudden shock, leaving a man feeling that the purpose has been taken out of his life. The death of old friends, or even more, of a spouse or sibling is clearly another. These events occur at a time when people are least well adapted to sudden changes in circumstances, and they constitute one of the peculiar problems of old age. A feeling of loneliness is more a function of desolation than of isolation. A single old person who has lived for many years by herself is less likely to say she feels lonely than a widow whose bereavement has only recently occurred, or than a man recently deprived of the companionship of his workmates, even though, comparatively, both may be richly provided with relatives and friends.

The family

One thing is certain – most of these problems will be

[1] I. M. Richardson *Age and need* Livingstone, 1964.

contained within the family. The task of the social services is to supplement the family system of care, where necessary, and to provide more extensive help to those without living children, or whose relatives are unable – or in rare instances unwilling – to assist. This does not mean, however, that old people should be expected to live with their children when they become a little infirm. There is substantial evidence that the majority of them would rather not do so, if it can be avoided. They want to be near their relatives but not actually on top of them. Likewise, they would prefer to remain in their own homes rather than go into an institution. Fortunately, both aims are accepted policy: in its report on the National Health Service the Guilleband Committee stated, in relation to old age, that the 'first aim should be to make adequate provision for the treatment and care of old people in their own homes'.[1]

The social services

A policy, however, is not necessarily an actuality. How far do the social services measure up to the tasks they have set themselves? Before evaluating this a more precise statement on the kinds of needs that the services can meet, or help to meet, is necessary. The most important is perhaps the provision of an adequate income; for without that no form of independent existence is possible. Secondly, and little less vital, comes accommodation for the able-bodied: suitable housing for old people. Next comes the whole range of services intended to provide medical care and social support in the home – including here the important function of scouting or screening for other agencies. Fourthly, there is short-term hospital treatment in hospital. Finally there is the provision of accommodation for those who have become too frail to

[1] Ministry of Health. *Report of the Committee of Enquiry into the cost of the National Health Service* (Guillebaud Committee) H.M.S.O., 1956. Cmnd. 9663. paragraph 647.

look after themselves in their own homes – residential hostels and long-term geriatric care in hospitals. It will be noticed that with the exception of the last none of these needs is peculiar to the elderly.

Let us take them in order. There is no space here to deal in any detail with the complicated question of ensuring financial security for old people, but a few points are essential. Pensioners have shared in the increasing prosperity of the country. Indeed, the researches of Lambert into nutrition,[1] using the results of the National Food Surveys, suggest that the greatest poverty is now to be found among large families; the diet of old people has improved over the past ten years. On the other hand, the old age pension for a single person, together with an average National Assistance allowance for rent, amounted in 1955 to 18 per cent of average earnings. Ten years later the proportion was almost precisely the same, although the latest increases (to a basic pension of £4) will somewhat improve the relative position of old people.

As for National Assistance, there is some evidence that the Board's officers are rather more generous in their interpretation of the regulations than a few years ago: between 1960 and 1963 there was a slight increase in the proportion of pensioners who received a 'discretionary addition' as part of their allowance. In many areas winter fuel allowances seem to be given almost automatically, given the age and general physical state of the applicant. But there are still significant regional and local differences in practice, and however humane the administration may be, the fact remains that there are quite a few old people eligible for National Assistance and not receiving it. Cole and Utting calculated that 12 per cent of their sample were in this position – which would represent over 800,000 pensioners in England and Wales. Many

[1] R. Lambert *Nutrition in Britain 1950–60* Welwyn: Codicote P., 1964.

old people feel that Assistance is a form of charity and an insult to their pride; the elderly still often call National Assistance 'Public Assistance,' and many put off applying while they have savings, however small.

Housing

Second only in importance to income is the provision of suitable accommodation. As a group, old age pensioners, particularly those who live alone, occupy the worst housing. They are more likely to live in privately rented accommodation than other sections of the community, and many of their homes have the generally poor standard of equipment typical of such housing. The Rowntree study,[1] for instance, found that 38 per cent of 'older small households' possessed no fixed bath, compared with 29 per cent of all households. Similar proportions were noted for other standard amenities. Far too many pensioners too, live in first or second floor flats or rooms in old houses without lifts. A lot of them have great difficulty in managing stairs, and their situation is very difficult when, as so often happens, both the coal and the nearest lavatory are in the yard several flights below. In general, older people are not overcrowded: the Rowntree investigators found that 38 per cent of pensioner households possessed three rooms per person or more, while the figure for the population as a whole was only 13 per cent. This abundance of space can be a problem in itself: when elderly people become frail the task of keeping a big house or flat clean can be crippling – especially if the property is old.

Richardson, in his study of North-East Scotland,[2] made estimates of housing need which represented a compromise between the observations of the researchers, (based on such objective criteria as sanitary facilities), and

[1] D. V. Donnison, C. Cockburn and T. Corlett *Housing since the Rent Act* Welwyn: Codicote, P., 1961

[2] I. M. Richardson, *op cit.*

the expressed wishes of the old people interviewed (quite a few of those occupying unsuitable property evinced no desire to move, especially in the country districts). In Aberdeen city, 7 per cent of those in the professional and managerial classes, 15 per cent of those in the skilled manual and routine non-manual classes, and 28 per cent of those in the semi-skilled and unskilled manual classes, were judged to need re-housing.

Until recent years this was not a problem which public authorities were able to meet: they inevitably concentrated on providing family-style housing for families. In 1956, local authorities were building about 15,000 one-bedroom dwellings a year: in 1963 the total was not far short of 35,000. However, not all these dwellings will be occupied by old people, and 35,000 does not look so impressive when set against the estimate of the National Corporation for the Care of Old People, that 75,000 a year are needed.

In recent years, a good deal of attention has been paid to the idea of providing sheltered housing for old people. This kind of accommodation would normally consist of a group of self-contained flatlets, which possesses some communal facilities and the services of a warden. Such schemes have the great advantage that the independence of the residents is assured, but assistance is 'on tap' if it is required. By March 1963, however, in about half of the counties and county boroughs in England and Wales there was either no such housing at all, or less than three persons aged 65 and over in every thousand were housed in this way.

There is a basic ambiguity in the public provision of housing for old people. It is intended to serve two largely separate purposes, all too often not kept distinct – first, to build dwellings which are more suitable for the elderly than conventional houses; secondly to make conventional houses now occupied by old people available to families with young children, and thus to reduce 'under occupation'. The first aim can best be met through sheltered housing, the second by the provision of one or two bedroomed dwellings, which could just as well be called accommodation for the over 55's, since by that age most couples no longer share accommodation with their children. In either case, all new housing likely to be inhabited by the elderly should meet certain specifications. Far too many local authorities are still installing conventional-type baths, and far too few provide handrails and similar aids.

Domiciliary services

To turn to the domiciliary services. Tunstall found that 17 per cent of the 538 pensioners he interviewed had seen their G.P. in the previous week; 4.5 per cent had been assisted by a home help; 1.3 per cent received meals-on-wheels and 1.7 per cent had been paid a visit by a Health Visitor, home nurse or visitor to the blind. Similar proportions have been found by other researchers. The General Practitioner has the widest coverage. But the fact remains that quite a few elderly people see their doctor very rarely: the comparative international survey found 30 per cent, and in Lewisham Amelia Harris found 20 per cent of all respondents had not consulted their G.P. in the past year. And the coverage of the other services is considerably lower: even if lunch clubs are added to meals on wheels a maximum of 2 per cent have this kind of help; and even if private domestic help is taken together with the local authority service then a maximum of around 14 per cent receives regular paid assistance with housework.

To put this in perspective we have already said that a high proportion of old people do not require help, and of those that do, much of it will be given by members of their family. Is there then any problem? Might not the admittedly small number of people receiving the social services represent the total of those needing them?

Unfortunately, there is plenty of evidence to suggest that this is not so. The home help service will serve as an example. The international survey showed that about 5 – 7 per cent would like to have a home help but were not being serviced now. Richardson estimated, on the basis of a purely socio-medical assessment, that about 3 per cent in North-East Scotland needed domestic help, but were not receiving any.

The picture is very similar for other services – too few chiropodists, too few home nurses, too few meals-on-wheels, vans, drivers and helpers. Far too many old people fail to get their eyes regularly retested; some of them are wearing spectacles handed down from their fathers, or which were dispensed for them thirty years previously. Nor is the quality of service always as it should be. Meals-on-wheels are rarely delivered more than twice a week to a house; and those who cannot cook for themselves and have no home help presumably either have to make their 'meat and two veg' last over the remainder of the week, rely on neighbours and relatives, or live on bread and cheese. Moreover, practically all the services go into hibernation over the week-end.

The family doctor

Deficiencies may be particularly serious in services which sift, and pass on cases to other agencies. Of prime importance here are the General Practitioners. Yet there is plenty of evidence that they are unaware of some medical conditions which occur among their elderly patients, including some major ones. Williamson and his associates studied a random sample of 200 over-65's on the lists of three general practitioners in practice in and around Edinburgh.[1] The men had a mean of 3.26 disabilities of which 1.87 were unknown to their G.P.; women a mean of 3.42 disabilities of which 2.03 were unknown. It was

[1] James Williamson *et el Old people at home: their unreported needs* The Lancet, 23 May 1964, p. 1117.

considered that no less than 59 of the 200 would have benefited from the services of a hospital specialist.

Such figures are disturbing: though criticism of the family doctor should be muted. Doctors with 2,400 patients on their list, and an average of perhaps $5\frac{1}{2}$ consultations a year with each of them, cannot be expected to give the maximum desirable quality of service to all their elderly patients. The real trouble, as the Royal College of Physicians at Edinburgh in a report on the 'Care of the Elderly in Scotland' points out, is that self-reporting of illness, which seems to work well enough with younger age-groups, is simply not adequate as a means of locating the medical conditions of elderly people.

The health visitor

In the circumstances the role of the Health Visitor could be crucial. As a nurse, she is well-placed to spot physical ailments, and as a local authority employee trained in the structure and functions of the welfare services, she should be able to refer people to the appropriate non-medical agencies. Unfortunately, far too many General Practitioners appear to know little about her job. Williamson and his associates estimated that 26 men and 50 women would benefit from the service of the Health Visitor, but discovered only 3 men and 2 women who had received them.[1] Part of the trouble is that very little of the time of the average Health Visitor is taken up with the elderly. The Edinburgh Royal College of Physicians found that in none of the forty Scottish Health Authorities from which they received details did Health Visitors spend more than 20 per cent of their time on the care of old people, and in 17 of them less than five per cent of their time was devoted to this kind of visiting. It is to be hoped that experiments in which Health Visitors are attached to group practices, or to a number of

[1] James Williamson, *op cit.*

individual doctors working on their own account, will become much commoner.

Meanwhile, much of the task of assessment and referral for non-medical services (including chiropody) passes to other hands. Some local authorities use their Welfare Officers (from the Welfare Department) on this task. More commonly, the job is allocated to no-one in particular. It should however, be pointed out that National Assistance Board officers go into over 20 per cent of old people's homes, and quite a large number of referrals may come through them. In Lewisham it was found that those in receipt of National Assistance were both better informed about the services available, and were more likely to use them.

The hospitals

The hospitals also represent another important source of referrals. This is not surprising, since the policy of rapid turnover pursued by the growing number of active geriatric units, depends upon adequate domiciliary care; and if the services are not available, the result will be blocked beds, clinically unnecessary admissions, or hasty readmissions. The majority of old people going into hospital enter acute wards and not geriatric wards, contrary to popular belief; but the latter take the more severely deteriorated patients, often on a long-term basis. Long-term accommodation is also provided by local authorities in residential hostels (or old people's homes).

Both local authorities and Hospital Management Committees have received a depressing legacy in out-of-date buildings, usually old Poor Law institutions: Sheldon has described the slum conditions prevailing in some of the hospitals in the West Midland Region,[1] and Townsend has given an even more scarifying account of

[1] J. H. Sheldon *Report to the Birmingham Regional Hospital Board on its geriatric service* The Board, 1961.

some of the local authority hostels still in use.[1] The latest figures (as at the end of 1963) show that 24,600 of the 73,000 odd old people living in homes directly run by English and Welsh local authorities were in hostels containing more than 70 beds. In fact this means, more often than not, that they live in old institutions along with probably 250 fellow residents, and bright new floor coverings can do little to relieve the gloom of these petty Bastilles. There has, however, been a gradual improvement: in 1960, when Townsend wrote, almost exactly half of the total accommodation provided by local authorities in England and Wales was in old Public Assistance Institutions: now the proportion must be about a third. About 400 of the 1,550 local authority homes were purpose-built between 1945 and the end of 1963.

This brief survey has tended to become a catalogue of deficiencies. It should be remembered that, inadequate though the British domiciliary services may often seem they are superior to those prevailing in most other developed countries. Furthermore, many of the difficulties arise from the shortages of trained staff: for example the hospitals, the health visiting services, and the home nursing service are all in competition for scarce qualified nurses.

The need for change

What sort of arrangements within local authorities would best serve the interest of the old? Some authorities place the welfare services under the Medical Officer of Health; others have a separate Welfare Department with its own Chief Officer. Which is the more desirable arrangement is a vexed question, and the answer to it may differ from place to place. The advantage in having separate departments is that it can then operate as *the* recognized department for old people, one place to which they can go

[1] Peter Townsend *The last refuge* Routledge, 1962.

for a variety of different kinds of help. A few local authorities already organize their services with this end in view. Salford, for instance, keeps a register of older people in the borough. All those on the list are visited periodically by welfare officers, who are thus able to keep an eye on changing circumstances. A further modification involves the transfer of the home help service to the Welfare Department: only one authority (Coventry) has taken this obvious step so far. The service was started primarily in order to cater for mothers at the time of childbirth, but as time has passed, it has become more and more a service for the old and infirm.

Voluntary effort

What part do, and should, voluntary bodies play in the general pattern of services? The first essential is clearly that voluntary effort should be co-ordinated, and here the role of local old people's welfare committees is crucial. Their organization and outlook differ somewhat from one area to the next. Kathleen Slack, in her study in inner London, found that these ranged from those which were virtually adjuncts of the local authority to those which were run by people regarding themselves as the guardians of the voluntary principle and who kept statutory agencies at arm's length. Both extremes seem highly undesirable but it seems clear these committees should maintain their independence: professional and voluntary are not antithetical terms. What this means in practice is a trained (and probably paid) organizer who will be able to deploy the voluntary assistance available to the best advantage. At present 'most old people's welfare committees work on shoestring budgets, without proper offices, and depending on the devoted services of part-time voluntary secretaries. Many of these committees can only do a proportion of what they would wish to do.'[1] In these circumstances the grants given for

[1] National Old People's Welfare Council. *Annual Report, 1962.*

administrative purposes by the National Corporation for the Care of Old People to a few selected committees are a welcome experiment.

In which spheres is voluntary effort most appropriate? Some services, which call for an unofficial touch, are clearly suitable, for example the running of clubs for the elderly, or the regular visiting of lonely old people. The latter could prove a most valuable service, though in most of the areas in which it exists at all, it is on a minute scale. Apart from this distinction there can be no precise demarcation between the statutory and voluntary field. In general, services which require a large and constant stream of hard cash are best left to statutory agencies. But they can be pioneered by voluntary bodies and then handed onto the local authority as a going concern: chiropody is a good example of a service that has developed in this way. The voluntary organization is then able to switch its resources to spotlighting a few more of the gaps in official provision. It follows from this that a lively Old People's Welfare Committee will see one of its most important tasks as being experimental.

For example several Committees have pioneered the idea of 'boarding out' suitable old people with families. Such schemes were first started in Exeter and Plymouth, and at the latest count, there were 29 of them in existence, some run by old people's welfare committee's and some by local authorities. Another appropriate field for experimentation – very neglected in this country compared to the United States – is preparation for retirement. Well planned and integrated schemes, supported by local industry are needed. Only a handful exist to date; perhaps the best known and most successful is in Glasgow, where much of the incentive has come from one firm (Rolls Royce).

Day care

Another area where much needs doing, and not so

much has been done, is day care. Here the hospitals and local authorities, as well as voluntary organizations, have plenty of scope. In St Pancras a most interesting scheme was started in 1961. The aim was to help those old people who, through infirmity or slight mental confusion, were unfit to be alone for long periods, had no wish to enter hospital or a hostel, and needed more assistance than existing domiciliary services, statutory or voluntary, could give. In the first fifteen months, 127 people were found who could benefit from service (out of 234 referred by other agencies, and investigated by the organizer: assessment was careful). Their needs were met in two ways: by appointing 'good neighbours' who would look in, and chat with, the old person, perhaps three times a day, and through 'sitters-up' who would relieve the strain on relatives by staying with their aged and infirm parents or grandparents for a few hours, half a day or a whole day, once a week. They would perform simple household tasks, such as cooking a light meal, if necessary. Both categories of helpers were paid for their trouble. It will be noted that one of the prime purposes of such schemes is to help relatives, quite as much as the old people themselves: and in view of what we said earlier about the sacrifices they may incur, the recognition that this is a task for the social services is a welcome development.

The future

In conclusion, we may say that it is unfortunate to treat the elderly as a homogeneous problem group, seeing them in isolation from their families and other younger members of their community.

Welfare agencies, voluntary and statutory services should attempt to provide a diversity of services, tailored to the diversity of demands and needs that exist. This means using social research methods to find out what the elderly want. A survey might find, for instance, that 75 per cent of the old people wanting rehousing in a town would like to live in houses interspersed among family dwellings on an estate: while 25 per cent favoured the idea of living in a group with other old people. Such results should, surely, be determining factors when local councils decide on their housing programme. Not that this is a simple matter of market research; old people may be confused about their wants, and it is difficult to choose if the alternatives are not clearly known. 'Granny flats' for instance – self contained dwellings attached to the houses occupied by sons or daughters – might prove very popular: but to find that out, experimentation would be necessary. Thus, a lively local authority would want bungalows, accommodation in tall flats, conversions of existing houses, sheltered housing schemes with wardens, and all, catering for differing preferences. Similar variety and experimentation is required in the other services. Britain has not been backward in providing services to meet diverse needs, but a good deal more needs to be done.

Medical social work

DENISE H. ZIMAN

Until fairly recently, medical social workers were known as almoners, and their decision to take on a new title marks a significant change in attitude to their work. At one time working exclusively in the hospitals, they are now moving out into the wider community, to work alongside other professional social workers.

Mrs Ziman trained as a medical social worker at the London School of Economics and at the Institute of Almoners. She worked in both general and teaching hospitals until 1957 when she took the Advanced Casework Course at the Tavistock Clinic. A year later she was appointed Unit Supervisor at the Middlesex Hospital, in charge of students from the Applied Social Studies Course of the London School of Economics who were doing their fieldwork placements there. She is currently part-time editor of *Medical Social Work*.

Medical social workers, who until October 1964 were called almoners, have always been concerned with the social and personal problems that so often accompany sickness and disability and with the prevention of waste of available medical care. The emphasis of their work has varied as the social and administrative preoccupations in the community have shifted.

In the last quarter of the nineteenth century hospitals were struggling with the age-old problem of selecting the 'deserving' cases from the growing mass of applicants for care. Charles Loch, General Secretary of the Charity Organization Society which had been formed to rationalize the giving of charity, campaigned to do something about the abuse of medical charities which was then rife particularly in the out-patient departments of hospitals.

The social workers

The pioneers

It was thought many of the applicants could make provision for their own medical care, and the Royal Free Hospital agreed to allow a Charity Organization Society social worker to attempt over three months to devise an equitable method of selecting those who needed and could benefit from medical care, and who could not by their own efforts obtain it in any other way. The social worker was Mary Stewart, and her appointment in 1895 marks the beginning of the profession of medical social workers, which today numbers some 1,300 active members.

Mary Stewart's primary task was to prevent the abuse of the hospital by those who could afford to pay, to weed out those whose needs would be more appropriately met through the Poor Law, and to encourage all those who could afford to do so to join a Provident Dispensary. Being a social worker fully conversant with the problems of the day which beset the poorer classes, she interpreted 'to prevent the abuse of the hospital' widely, to include ensuring that the care it gave those who qualified for it was not wasted through ignorance or preventible poverty.

Gradually the advantages of appointing a social worker to help control the pressure on the hospital's resources became evident, and from Mary Stewart's initial experimental appointment until just before the outbreak of the first World War, about twenty hospitals added the new 'lady almoners' to their establishments. Increasingly their time was spent on combatting ignorance, overcoming poverty and helping patients by every means that could be devised to rise above their circumstances, and to strengthen their self-respect and capacity for self-reliance. Before the establishment of the maternity and child welfare clinics and the development of a comprehensive health visitor service, almoners did what they could to tackle the problems of the tuberculous, by education, by the improvement of hygiene and diet, by arrangement for care in sanatoria. They established ante and post-natal clinics to ward off the worst of preventible complications and to try to secure a healthier start in life for the babies; later they strove to instil the basic principles of health and hygiene into the mothers of young children, in order to promote health as well as prevent disease.

They continued to study the needs of the sick and disabled throughout the first World War and the slump years that followed it. As the pinch of the economic crisis affected the subscriptions to the voluntary hospitals, a system of payment according to means was introduced, and almoners became increasingly involved in this assessment. The pressure of administrative duties grew, leaving less and less time and energy for the social work aspect of their work, which almoners always thought should be their main concern.

The second World War added more administrative pressure because of the problems of evacuation and of the Emergency Medical Service. Perhaps partly in order to reassure themselves that they had not been quite cut off from their social work roots, almoners thrashed out during those years the basic principles on which medical social work has grown, and evolved a training which linked practical experience of social problems accompanying illness with the fast-developing fields of sociology, psychology, social administration and medicine itself.

National Health Service

After the advent of the National Health Service in 1948, a Memorandum issued by the Minister of Health to hospitals management committees, emphasized the fact that almoners were to be regarded as medical social workers with a recognized place in the treatment team.

The social workers

Their duties were properly to include '(i) social investigation and interviews to provide understanding of the social and personal background of the patient, and in particular to give the doctor information which is relevant to diagnosis and treatment; (ii) social action to minimize personal anxieties, family difficulties and other problems during illness; (iii) the making of arrangements with the local health authorities concerned with the home visiting of patients who may for a time, or in some instances for a long period, need help to ensure that the value of their treatment is not lost.'

The National Health Service cleared away at one stroke the necessity for almoners to be involved with payment for treatment. Now they were, theoretically at least, free to concentrate on what they and the Minister of Health considered to be their proper social work function – that of dealing with the many different problems arising from and contributing to illness.

But this also brought them face to face with the task of persuading doctors and administrators, both in hospitals and in local authorities, to use their services appropriately. It meant that they could no longer hide, as some had been tempted to do, behind an administrative justification of their existence in order to carry out their less easily accepted social work functions unobserved and unopposed. From the very beginning, almoners were seen with mixed feelings by doctors and nurses alike. Some were convinced that they had a useful contribution to make to the total care of the sick; others feared encroachment of their particular spheres of activity and influence, and possibly a curtailment of their power. As medicine develops and as the intimate connections between the state of a person's mind, his emotions, his social and material environment and his state of physical health have become more and more evident, greater recognition is being given to the importance of social and emotional factors in the management of illness and

116

disability. This in turn makes it easier for the medical social workers to fulfil their proper roles as social workers in a medical setting.

Underlying their work today is still the old aim 'the prevention of wastage of available medical care', but interpreted somewhat differently. Now the aim is to resolve as far as possible any difficulty – material, personal or emotional – which might prevent the patient from seeking the care he needs, or from co-operating fully in his treatment. The aim is still to help people to retain the greatest degree of independence that their circumstances will permit.

The Minister of Health in his Memorandum in 1948 had a comprehensive grasp of the range of services a medical social worker might call upon to help patients. The kinds of problems that beset people when they become sick or have an accident vary greatly according to their circumstances and to the implications of the illness. A wage-earner may face a reduction in income, or if the illness is severe he may need to take up a totally new and more suitable kind of work. The mother of young children may be temporarily unable to look after them. An old person may never again be able to live alone. Less obvious difficulties that can arise stem from the possible emotional responses to illness and disablement. Invariably the sick have to cope with some degree of anxiety and uncertainty; often treatments are painful and fear may be acute; the change of status involved on becoming a sick, and so to some extent a dependent, person may be difficult to bear. For everyone illness or disablement involves a greater or lesser degree of disruption of the usual pattern of living, and whether or not the medical social worker's services are needed to help resolve the social and economic problems which arise depends on a great number of factors. Many people, thanks to their social, economic and emotional security, are able to cope without professional help. Others cannot manage, and then appropriate help from the medical social worker may limit the social and emotional consequences of their illness and ensure a speedier and more complete return to independence when it is over.

Methods

Medical social workers, in common with other social workers use the casework method. A careful study of the patient, of his social environment, of his hopes and fears, strengths and weaknesses, is nearly always necessary if he is to be helped appropriately and effectively.

As in the past, medical social workers are today still concerned to ensure that patients and their families do not lack the basic material essentials. This may mean advising them how to draw the benefits which the State provides, such as sickness benefit, disability pensions, National Assistance Board allowances, and so on. Statutory provisions on the whole ensure a basic subsistence level, but between this and a tolerable level of living there is frequently a gap which can only be filled, and that to a limited extent, by the use of voluntary charitable resources. The medical social worker needs an exhaustive knowledge of all the many sources of help that exist for people who are ill or disabled, and she must be able to put her patient in touch with whatever organization may be able to fill his need appropriately.

Material help

Sometimes material help brings relief to the family of a sick person and sometimes its secondary, psychological, effect of comfort and encouragement serves to keep a family going in the face of long-term hardship and depression. In the case of Mr Adams, this sort of help was really all that could be offered. He had been unemployable for three years following a severe head injury sustained at work. His three children were still at school and the family's finances were very tight. The brunt of running the family's affairs and coping with her husband's moods of depression which alternated with periods of violent temper, fell on Mrs Adams. He had suffered a personality change as a result of his accident, but neither his children nor the neighbours really appreciated this, so that they tended to think he was making the most of his injuries and were not as helpful nor as sympathetic as Mrs Adams would have wished. Faced with a court order to pay 10s a week to clear a hire purchase account which they had undertaken when Mr Adams was earning well as a fitter, Mrs Adams finally accepted the doctor's recommendation that she should discuss her problems with the medical social worker. This went against the grain since both she and her husband were very bitter about having to ask for help of any sort. She was particularly hurt when, on the rare occasions that she did ask for special supplementary help, the National Assistance Board officer had been forced to investigate both her need and her means before meeting her claim. She interpreted this scrutiny as grudging her charity and, when she saw the medical social worker, she expected the same approach and was therefore somewhat defensive and hostile.

She was mollified by the medical social worker's frank recognition of the size of her task. Providing she kept rigidly to her budget week in week out Mrs Adams said she could just about manage. But she felt very discouraged. She could never afford to spend half a crown impulsively and Christmas she really dreaded. The knowledge that she had years of this pinching and scraping ahead of her and that she could not hope for her husband to improve either physically or mentally sometimes overwhelmed her so that she felt like giving up.

The medical social worker knew that Mrs Adams needed real encouragement and support at this juncture to enable her to carry on. She was already receiving all the help available from statutory sources, so an appeal was made to two trust funds to clear the outstanding debt and for a lump sum to be spent exactly as Mrs Adams wished. A total of £60 was raised and in addition the three children were offered summer holidays through the Children's Holiday Fund. Mrs Adams was immensely cheered by the spontaneity of the gifts, feeling that her capacity as a good manager had been recognized. She admitted she had been sinking deeper into a state of depression and thought this in turn had made her less able than before to spin the money out. The medical social worker, seeing her isolation from the stimulus of social contacts, put Mrs Adams in touch with the local Townswomen's Guild and left it that Mrs Adams would approach her again if she should find herself once more overwhelmed by all her domestic responsibilities.

In this case, no very fundamental change in the family's basic situation could be brought about because of the hard facts of Mr Adams' disability which were irreversible and inescapable. Mrs Adams would have for years to struggle on somehow. But she had been helped over a period of crisis when her problems threatened to overcome her completely.

Adjusting to illness

Illness frequently entails loss of some kind. Loss of energy, loss of physical power, loss of ability, loss of status. It frequently leads to feelings of depression or anxiety in the patient and his normal way of dealing with stress of any sort will certainly be disturbed. His reactions to these feelings may further complicate life for him by blinding him to the true facts of his situation and making it difficult for him to react appropriately. This in turn may set off a third wave of complications which may not only affect his social situation but may adversely affect his response to the medical care offered to him. Medical social workers are therefore on the alert to detect signs of depression or other emotional reaction to illness, so as to reduce its effects as far as possible.

The case of Mr Bolton illustrates this very closely. He was a widower, aged 73, who had diabetes and osteo-arthritis of the knees and hips. The doctor recommended him to have a wheel-chair to make him more mobile in the hope that this would combat his evident depression. Mr Bolton's unwillingness to co-operate caused the doctor to ask the medical social worker to see what lay behind this attitude. Increasing difficulty in getting about coupled with deteriorating health had resulted, a year before, in Mr Bolton's firm finally insisting on his retiring. He had clung to his job as a clerk long after the normal retirement age simply because he could not face life without it. He had led a cheerless existence since his wife's death thirteen years ago, daily dreading retirement because it would lock him up in his loneliness. When his firm had eventually retired him he felt, despite all the gifts and the farewell party that had been arranged for him, that he was being rejected as a worthless shell of a man, and he withdrew hurt and bewildered, refusing to respond to the friendly gestures of his colleagues. His resentment soured him; he growled at his friends and neighbours so that he alienated them; he found himself alone and neglected and this confirmed his feeling that in his old age people were ready to toss him aside. He argued this was because he could no longer do what he used to do for others, and so assumed that their friendship for him had been self interest.

In this bitter, disillusioned state of mind, living alone on a small pension, grappling with increasing pain and immobility, the dietary restrictions imposed by diabetes appeared to be the final blow. He sought solace by indulging in the sweet but forbidden foods, and inevitably his physical condition deteriorated. He neglected his appearance and his home reflected his depression and lassitude. His one remaining contact with the outside world was his connection with the church, and this too, because of his depression, was in danger of breaking down.

Understandably, he was not interested in the doctor's recommendation that he should have a self-propelled wheel-chair. He thought that by urging him to activity at the age of 73 the doctor was implying that he was loafing. The medical social worker encouraged Mr Bolton to talk out all these feelings of resentment, and expressed concern about the impoverished life he saw currently being forced to lead. She gave him the opportunity to tell her about incidents in his life which showed he had once been a vigorous and effective man. Gradually, as her concern warmed him and his physical state began to yield to treatment, Mr Bolton recovered from his depression. His more cheerful attitude communicated itself to others so that they in turn reacted more positively towards him. Mr Bolton began to co-operate more whole-heartedly in his treatment and became eager to have the wheel chair recommended for him. He accepted the services of a home help and finally decided to turn the upper floor into a flat for a middle-aged couple who would, as he put it, 'break up the echoes' in the house. Finally, when the local vicar asked him to take on the church accounts, Mr Bolton felt he still had a valid contribution to make to life and joked that he threatened to be busier in retirement than he had been before.

It is not uncommon to find that people, through dread of a possible development, react in precisely the way calculated to bring it about. Mr Bolton was so afraid of retirement that he actually aggravated his physical ills by his struggles. The medical social worker was able to intervene and by helping him to make good use of the medical care available to him helped him to go on leading a satisfying life at home. It was necessary to uncover the feelings of deprivation and depression which underlay Mr Bolton's refusal to co-operate in his treatment before the doctor and physiotherapist could make much headway with him.

Sometimes the obstacle to effective treatment lies in the secondary gain that can be obtained from an illness, where the immediate disadvantages, such as pain or limited activity, may be outweighed by the hold it gives the patient on his relatives, whom he may fear would otherwise neglect him. Where a person's social or emotional situation is so impoverished that the secondary gains of the illness have real value for him he may feel he risks losing more than he can afford by losing his illness. The medical social worker has to discover for what needs the patient is trying to compensate, and to help him find more appropriate ways of doing so before he will engage in co-operating fully in his treatment. Facing up to the feelings aroused by illness or loss is immensely important if secondary repercussions are to be avoided. The time to face the feelings and deal with them appropriately is ideally at the time they first come up, that is to say, at the point of crisis when the patient is ill and being treated. Failing this it is sometimes possible at a subsequent point of crisis to help the patient resolve feelings left over from a previous experience which are hampering him. There can be no short cuts to working through emotional upheavals and the failure to do so adequately can have far-reaching effects.

Susan Robinson was the victim of such a situation. She had lost her first baby at birth after an unexpectedly difficult labour and delivery. She and her soldier husband, married for two years, had epitomized the ideal of a happy young couple embarking on parenthood. Everything at home was ready to greet the baby and everyone, staff and relatives alike, was aghast at the tragic shattering of the happiness of the couple. The doctor told Mrs Robinson gently but firmly when she recovered consciousness that her baby had died, not encouraging her to dwell on it, and quickly gave her more sedatives, advising her to concentrate on recovering so that she would soon be fit to try again.

Her husband, meanwhile, was exhorted not to allow his wife to dwell on their loss and to encourage her to take up normal life again as soon as possible. When Mrs Robinson got home, she found the flat re-decorated, all trace of the nursery removed, all the baby equipment gone. She expressed surprise, but was urged by her husband and relatives to put all that behind her. She had said little in hospital about the loss of her baby, and now she carried on trying to forget. She returned to her job and her husband went back to his regiment.

Eighteen months later, Mrs Robinson returned to hospital pregnant again. She attended the ante-natal clinic regularly but apart from this did nothing to prepare for the baby's birth. She went on working and as the pregnancy progressed it was noted in the clinic that, although physically she was well, she looked increasingly pale and tired. Finally the doctor sent her to the medical social worker, ostensibly to make sure that she would have plenty of help available to her in the few weeks before and after the baby was born.

The medical social worker noted Mrs Robinson's lack of interest in planning the future. She therefore turned her attention to the present, and drew Mrs Robinson out about how she was feeling and how she was managing the waiting months. A reference to the fact that she must be feeling anxious about the outcome of this pregnancy in view of the last met with a bland denial, and the first interview ended with Mrs Robinson agreeing to come again should she need help, while the medical social worker felt very concerned about her evident depression and apathy.

A month later, Mrs Robinson, looking even more wan and tired, saw the medical social worker again, this time apparently wanting to talk. Given an opening to say how she felt, she revealed that she was very unhappy.

She and her husband had been quarrelling in the last years so that they now both dreaded his leaves. Yet she felt terribly lonely when he was not there and had nightmares, the theme of which was always to do with losing and with fruitless searching. She could take no interest in anything. She could take no pleasure in the thought of having a child, although she did not suppose her previous experience of losing it at birth would be repeated. She found it distressing not to be able to work up any feelings about the new baby at all, and she was very afraid that she would not be able to love it when it came.

As she talked, it became obvious that Mrs Robinson did not dare to let herself feel about anything. She showed fear and bewilderment about the loss of her first child, being unable to grasp that it had actually been born, had died and had been buried. Never seeing it, never discussing its loss, and finding no trace of all the preparations they had made for it at home, had left her with a nightmarish feeling of unreality. Gradually this had spilt over into other areas in her life and she did not really believe in anything or care about anything. She felt alone and bereft and longed for her husband's company to dispel her misery, only to find when she did have it that they could not get near each other.

Mrs Robinson admitted that she would have liked to talk about the loss of her baby, but that she had not done so for fear of upsetting her husband and relatives. All this repressed anxiety and grief was being pushed to the fore again by the imminence of the new birth, and the medical social worker suggested that what Mrs Robinson needed was a chance to talk the previous experience out of her system. For several weeks Mrs Robinson continued to voice her feelings and anxieties, both about her loss, and about her present unhappiness with her husband. Gradually she seemed to gain some relief from her depression, and one day she asked whether her husband could come, since she thought he, too, would appreciate the chance to talk about his side of the story. Mr Robinson commented on the recent change in his wife's behaviour, admitting he had been really worried by her lack of interest in the expected baby, and that he was very anxious about her repeated attempts to rake over the ashes of their loss. The medical social worker explained Mrs Robinson's need to work through her feelings about the death of the first baby before being able to get involved emotionally with the second one, and went on to suggest that Mr Robinson too must have had his feelings to contend with. He made a wry comment about fathers being left out of these things, but went on to talk about his own reactions to the tragedy. At the end of a long interview he went away more relaxed and determined to let his wife talk.

The work of the medical social worker was nearly finished. Mrs Robinson had faced her reaction to her loss and the fears that stemmed from it about whether she would again be deprived of the baby she so much wanted. Her grief and depression, more overt now, were attached to their basic cause, and no longer spilling over every aspect of life for her. She and her husband were once again able to communicate freely, and she found that he understood her fears and could give her the warm support she needed to face the future. The doctors, meanwhile, had discovered how much this particular patient needed to be taken fully into their confidence, answering her questions as fully as they could.

In this case the secondary consequences of the patient's tragic experience were short-lived. Ideally, they should not have arisen in the first place, and it is fortunate that the incidence of some crisis centring round illness or disability can sometimes re-activate feelings, which the patient may have buried long ago, and which have gone on adversely affecting him in unsuspected ways, so that they become accessible to help.

The medical team

Always the medical social worker must work closely with the doctors and nurses concerned with treating the patient. This is obviously essential if the patient is to be treated as a whole person and not fragmented between different departments, each concentrating on helping their separate parts of him. It is obviously necessary, too, if social work care is to further the aim of medical treatment. There are other therapists whose contribution to the patient's treatment may be vital, and probably those people who face problems of major rehabilitation are the ones who occasion the most complicated network of co-operation, both within the hospital and with different organizations outside.

The medical social worker's contribution to the care of, for example, a newly chair-bound paraplegic, consists of studying the patient's background and assessing both his and his relatives' attitude to his illness and the need for total re-adjustment that results from it. She has to make this information available to the other people concerned in treating him, so that they may have as clear an understanding of their patient as possible to help them in their approach. She has, of course, to do what she can to help him come to terms with his situation, so as to be able to co-operate fully in his treatment. In trying to envisage what aids he will need at home she can count on the expert advice of the physiotherapist and the occupational therapist, both of whom may recommend appliances or structural alterations to the house to help the patient to be independent there. The local health and welfare authorities also have an important role to play here because they can arrange for these aids to be installed, and may well initiate such schemes for those people who are being cared for predominantly by their general practitioners and the community care services. The housing department of the local authority may be asked to allocate more suitable accommodation. The Ministry of Labour, through the local Disablement Resettlement Officer, will certainly be asked about re-employment, and this may involve a period of assessment at an Industrial Rehabilitation Unit followed by training for totally new work, if necessary, before the Ministry of Labour finally places the patient in employment again.

Those people facing chronic, long-term or progressive conditions may, from time to time, be confronted with changes in their circumstances which require adjustment, in much the same way as people facing an acute illness or the consequences of an accident. For them contact with a medical social worker can be a life-line, a way of having their changing needs appreciated, and of being put in touch with the help that is available to them in the community.

The community

With the growing tendency for the community to contain its own dependent members instead of catering for them in specialized institutions, the local authority health and welfare resources are expanding, and increasingly medical social workers are to be found working outside hospitals. At the same time there is a move for the closer integration of the local authority services and those provided by family doctors, and there are a growing number of group practices to which health visitors, midwives, and sometimes district nurses and medical social workers, are attached. In the years ahead it seems likely that hospitals will concentrate more on diagnosis and the treatment of acute phases of illness, while the general management of the sick and disabled will become increasingly the concern of the community health and welfare services. Medical social workers will still be needed in hospitals, but as their potential contribution to the care of the sick becomes more fully appreciated it is obvious they will have to work where the majority of the sick are to be found – in the community.

Medical social work

A medical social work service, wherever based, thrives best when the network of other services is adequate and well developed, because it depends so much on close and effective co-operation. The services available in any area differ because they are affected by historical development and local resources from place to place. How medical social workers are used today, whether employed by hospitals or by local authorities, also varies greatly from place to place, and for the same reasons. Just as in the early days, the attitude of the doctors towards the social and emotional factors in disease and towards the services intended to deal with them, has a big influence on the way the medical social service develops and on the nature of the work done.

Increasingly there is a tendency for local authorities to appoint medical social workers to help develop the skills of their workers in health and welfare departments, as well as using them in their own right to provide a medical social service. In this way it is hoped to ensure the existence of a comprehensive service to the sick and the disabled in the community. Currently the trouble lies in the acute shortage of trained medical social workers. This is due to a number of factors, most of which are common to all the service professions. Medical social work salaries, both for beginners and for those taking higher responsibilities, are not as attractive as those in some other fields. Training facilities, although they have increased as more universities have established courses for applied social studies, are still not enough to train all the people who could be absorbed.

In view of this shortage, which is likely to become more rather than less acute as the openings for medical social workers in the community continue to expand, it is particularly important that their services be used effectively. They cannot afford to spend their time on administrative duties which could be performed equally well by others without their training. They must do all they can to increase their professional competence and stream-line their methods of work, both in terms of organization and of technique, so as to make sure their intervention in the lives of the sick is as effective as possible.

For years medical social workers have been gradually moving away from a preoccupation about their function in the limited sphere of the hospital, becoming increasingly aware of the common ground they share with other social workers. The recent decision to drop the title almoner and to be known as medical social workers indicates their determination to emphasize their membership of the larger group of professional social workers. By developing the common links they have with other social work groups, and by moving out into the community, medical social workers will finally shake off the shackles which the events of two world wars and the intervening slump years bound round them.

Mental health

NOEL TIMMS

Noel Timms graduated in mediaeval history at London University, and then took a Diploma in Public and Social Administration at Oxford. He worked in a hostel for deprived children, and with problem families in Family Service Units in Liverpool and Birmingham. In 1955 he took the Diploma in Mental Health at the London School of Economics, and worked for two years in child guidance clinics in Surrey. At the present time he is a lecturer on the Mental Health and Applied Social Studies Course at the L.S.E. (where he also took an M.A. in Sociology).

His publications include *The problem of 'the problem family'* (with A. F. Philp) (1957), *Casework in the child care service* (1962), *Psychiatric social work in Great Britain* (1964), *Social casework: principles and practice* (1964), and *The Christian family in the mid-twentieth century* (1965).

Introduction

Questions of definition rarely add to the excitement of an introduction, but the meaning of the term 'mental health' is of more than the usual minor consequence.

In the broadest terms it would be possible to argue that all our social services come under the umbrella of mental health, since they could all be said to be aiming at maturity, adjustment and happiness. Indeed the mental hygiene movement of the 1930s commonly stressed such general objectives, and the origins in this country of the child guidance clinic, for example, at that time, are to be found in the belief that it is both meaningful and important to talk of 'mental hygiene' in the same way as we have become accustomed to emphasize 'physical hygiene'. As early as 1930 Wechsler, an American psychiatrist, warned that 'enthusiastic mental hygiene tells us that it is concerned with the prevention of mental deficiency, criminality, the psychoneuroses, the psychoses, anti-social traits, family unhappiness, divorce, prostitution, alcoholism, sexual perversion, epilepsy and other such simple matters.'[1] Taking a narrower definition, however, the mental health services can be seen as concerned not with achieving conditions of positive health but with the alleviation and cure of mental illness. Such questions of definition are not purely academic. They are at the heart of decisions about the future role of the local authority psychiatric services. Should these be concerned with the more general mental hygiene problems of the community or with those people who are likely to become, or have actually been, mental hospital patients?

Yet, whatever the faults of the mental hygiene movement it had the advantage of including within its scope consideration of what, before the Mental Health Act of 1959, used to be called mental deficiency. The 1959 Act was the first piece of legislation in this century to bring together provision for what are now termed the mentally subnormal and the severely subnormal and provision for the mentally ill. All these conditions are now known as 'mental disorder.' Ever since special provision was first made for the mentally subnormal the tendency has been for them to be regarded as the cinderella of the social services. In our new programmes for the mentally disordered it is important that due attention is given to the needs of the subnormal as well as the mentally ill.

Present policy – emphasis and origins

The essentials of our present policy for mental health revolve around five main principles:

(1) Mental illness is to be treated as far as possible like other forms of illness. This can be illustrated from

[1] I. S. Wechsler, quoted in Ginsburg, S. W. *A psychiatrist's views on social issues* Columbia U.P., 1963, p. 5.

the emphasis in Section 5 of the 1959 Mental Health Act on 'informal' admissions to 'any hospital or mental nursing home', and from the view of the Royal Commission on Mental Illness and Mental Deficiency (1954–7) that 'the division of functions between the local authorities, the hospitals, . . and other official bodies should be broadly the same in relation to mental disorder as in relation to other forms of illness or disability.' The notion that depression, for example, can be an illness has helped to remove the stigma attached to the old fashioned concept of 'madness'. It is always salutary to ask of any condition attached to the treatment of such a mental illness, why do we need it when we can treat physical illness without it? At the same time it is also important not to slide into the assumption that mental illness is the same as physical. It is not. Mental illness always involves our social behaviour and this is one of the reasons why it is more difficult to tolerate than physical illness. It also involves our own fears and fantasies much more vigorously, and this is one of the most crucial strains placed on the staff of the mental health services, whether they work in the local health authority, hospital or child guidance clinic.

(2) There are no longer two codes and two services for the mentally ill and the mentally defective. The very title of the 1959 Act embodies this principle, and the new procedures for application for a hospital place apply in the main to all types of disorder.

(3) The general social services available to the public at large should be available to the mentally disordered. Here the trend is away from the umbrella special service for a special isolated group. There are several examples of this in the 1959 Act. For instance, S.12 (i) gives authorities the power to compel the attendance of subnormal children at a Training Centre if they are of compulsory school age; S.9 (iii) permits the reception

133

into care by a local authority children's department of mentally disordered children.

(4) New emphasis should be given to the care of the mentally disordered in the community. Under the 1959 Act local health authorities were authorized (and later compelled by ministerial regulation) to use their powers to provide, equip and maintain residential accommodation; provide training centres; appoint mental welfare officers and exercise authority in relation to guardianship. This marked an extension of local authority work and the groups of people covered. In 1963, for example, local authorities in England and Wales provided 20 workshops or occupational centres for the mentally ill, serving some 390 people; by 1974 it is planned to provide 78 centres for nearly 3,000 people. Care in the community was a marked feature of local authority work with mental defectives after 1913, but the extension of this kind of work as a general feature of the local authority's responsibility is new.

(5) Many more patients should be cared for outside the hospital, and would be better for this. Such a principle must involve changes in the mental hospital, though what these changes are is not yet clear. Some see the hospital as able to re-define its role more along medical and less along custodial lines. Others see a danger of a situation in which the' bulk of present mental health work moves into the community services, and the mental hospital becomes an institution only for deteriorated long-stay patients to be treated by organic methods'.[1] Still others look forward to a considerable decline in the volume of work and importance of the mental hospital as an institution. What we are certainly witnessing is the growth of a more highly differentiated hospital service. The hospital service, depending on the area of one's residence, may offer extensive home visiting, day or night hospital care (by the end of 1959 there were 45 day hospitals),

[1] K. Jones *Mental health and social policy* Routledge, 1960.

or a hospital regime based on politics of 'the open door' and the 'therapeutic community'. This last development represents something of a revolution in hospital organization whereby 'treatment' is seen not as the very limited time spent with the psychiatrist in private interviews but as a product of 24-hour interaction between patients and staff.

The mental health services

These then seem to be the five main principles of change in our new mental health policy. But through what kind of services is this policy carried out?

THE CHILD GUIDANCE CLINIC. Chronologically the first line of defence against mental disorder is to be found in the child guidance clinics run by local authorities, and the child psychiatric clinics under the regional hospital boards. Present policy and fashion places such emphasis on community care for the adult that we tend perhaps to overlook the importance of the services offered to the child with the intention of preventing more extensive disturbance in his adult life.

In 1962 there were approximately 400 child guidance clinics and hospital psychiatric clinics for children. Some idea of their volume of work can be seen from the fact that in 1962 over 44,000 children were treated in the former, whilst the latter had a total of over 23,000 new cases. What each clinic counts as treament, however, probably varies according to the theoretical persuasion of staff, the number of staff available and the demands on their services. All clinics provide a service of diagnosis and treatment for disturbed children, but some will give priority to those under five years of age, others will concentrate on the long-term treatment of selected children. Very few clinics consider they can offer much help to the parents of subnormal children. We know, however, very little about the service in general and a full-scale national survey is long overdue.

The social workers

Traditionally, the child guidance service attempted to assess and treat children on the basis of the understanding and skill of the three disciplines represented in the 'ideal' clinic team, those of psychiatry, psychology and social work. Treatment was based originally on the assumption that the child would remain in his own home throughout its duration. However, there has gradually developed in this field a quite complex system of special educational provision for children ascertained as maladjusted. This includes special day and special boarding schools, hostels, home teaching and so on. This provision certainly plays an important part in helping disturbed children, but it has been suggested that the whole process of labelling children maladjusted and then providing separate services on this basis in fact contributes to keeping the child in a state of maladjustment.[1] Perhaps the most crucial question in this particular service concerns the future of the child guidance clinic. Will it develop generally, as it has done in certain parts of the country, into a psychiatric service for families with young children?

THE HOSPITAL. In 1948 the National Health Service inherited over 100 mental hospitals, but nearly half of these were built before 1891, and nearly a quarter before 1861. Almost half the patients in hospitals for the mentally defective were in institutions of more than 1,000 beds. Problems of size and kind of building are still pressing. In the Ten Year Plan[2] for hospitals published in 1962 region after region reported difficulties arising from the age and size and overcrowded conditions of their mental hospitals. The programmes in many hospitals today, with their emphasis on the participation of the patients and the consequent reliance on small groups, are

[1] R. Higgins *The concept of maladjustment: its social consequences* in *Human Relations* vol. 16, no. 1. 1963.

[2] Ministry of Health *A hospital plan for England and Wales* H.M.S.O., 1962. Cmnd. 1604.

not easily carried out in the buildings of an earlier age and disposition.

Two major problems confront the hospital service today: how do the staff respond to the new ideas of institutional treatment and to the newly emerging patterns of psychiatric care? The concept of treatment as an outcome of social interaction throughout the day questions the traditional division of roles between doctor, nurse and social worker. The doctor becomes perhaps the leader of a therapeutic team, with the nurse taking on the role of therapist rather than guardian and the social worker questioning whether she should not base her work outside rather than inside the institution. The basis of life within the hospital is also called into question. Should the hospital try to resemble as far as it can social life outside its walls or is its therapeutic effect based precisely on its difference from 'ordinary' social life? If the latter is the case, will the patient who has adjusted to life inside the hospital be able to cope with life outside?[1]

A number of connected trends have affected present patterns of care within the hospital. Firstly, there has been a substantial increase in admissions to mental hospitals, due perhaps to the growing acceptance of mental disturbance as an illness. Between 1949 and 1960 annual admissions to hospitals for mental illness rose by 59,000, more than doubling from 55,000 to 114,000 a year. Between 1951 and 1960 male first admission rates increased by 48 per cent and female rates by 54 per cent. Secondly, there has been a rapid increase in discharges, due to considerable advances in drug therapy. Between 1951 and 1960 male discharges increased by 117 per cent and female by 128 per cent. Thirdly, there is a general tendency for periods of hospital stay to become shorter. In 1952 29 per cent of the males

[1] This point is argued in R. Rapoport *Community as doctor* Tavistock, P . 1960.

discharged and 24 per cent of the females had been in hospital for less than 2 months; the figures for 1960 are 40 per cent and 35 per cent respectively. Fourthly, re-admission rates are rising: second admissions, for example, rose between 1951 and 1960 from 12,330 to 24,680. It would seem that there is a small but growing number of patients who are repeatedly admitted for one or two comparatively brief periods, and also of a group of long-stay permanently institutionalized patients. This last group should diminish, but at a slow rate. Even so, in 1959/60 it was found possible to discharge nearly 900 patients who had been in hospital continuously for a quarter of a century.

With regard to hospitals for the subnormal there has been much less change. The number of in-patients has gradually risen: the number of patients in hospitals for the subnormal was 10 per cent higher for males and 4 per cent for females in 1959 compared to 1951. The most noticeable increase has been amongst middle-aged and elderly defectives, admitted perhaps after the death of parents or other relatives. In 1960 there were about 60,000 defectives on the books of hospitals for the subnormal compared with about 55,000 in 1951. There are, however, very long waiting-lists for hospital accommodation. At the end of 1959 of the 6,000 or so cases waiting for admission half were classified as urgent. It is tempting to argue from the existing waiting lists that our most obvious need is for more of the hospitals for which there is such a clear demand. It is, however, important to consider possible alternatives to the building of large, costly institutions. Recent research suggests that a more appropriate model for the care of the subnormal child is the small, residential nursery.

LOCAL AUTHORITIES. At present local authorities provide a range of mental welfare services. In 1963, they ran nearly 400 training centres or social clubs for over

11,000 subnormal adults, 366 junior centres catering for about 16,600 children, 25 hostels for 484 subnormal adults and 17 junior hostels for 270 children. By 1974 there should be places for over 29,000 adult subnormals in the 631 training centres or clubs, for 25,000 children in the 423 junior centres, for over 7,000 in adult hostels and over 2,000 in 120 junior hostels. Similar increases are planned in the services for the mentally ill. In 1963 there were only 20 workshops or occupational centres for the mentally ill, 72 social centres and 20 hostels. By 1974 it is planned to provide 78 workshops for nearly 3,000 patients, 220 centres and 237 hostels. All these developments clearly require a considerable expansion in staff and also an extension of service in comparatively uncharted directions. Take the idea of the hostel for the mentally ill. How can the demand for these comparatively new institutions be assessed and for which age-ranges and groups of patients should they be provided? Are they short-stay, half-way homes between the hospitals and a fully independent life in the community, extensions of the hospital, or long-term residential units for cases not requiring active psychiatric treatment?

The most frequently emphasized service of the local authority in the field of mental disorder is, of course, its social work service. This is usually described quite simply as 'community care'. This term, however, is something of a battle cry, and battle cries are notorious for their imprecision. 'Community care' means different things to different people. To some it means care outside the hospital walls, on the apparent assumption that the hospital is somehow not in the community. To others it refers exclusively to a social work service rather than to a reorientation of the psychiatric services as a whole, whereby hospitalization is seen as one phase in the total provision of care for the patient. Finally, it is used as a synonym for the work of the local health authority, as if programmes of community care could not equally well be carried by hospitals.

The term 'community care' has come into use to describe the changed situation whereby, as we have seen, society is taking an increasing responsibility for a wide range of provision for mental disorder at a time when exclusive reliance on hospital or residential care is being questioned on a number of practical and theoretical grounds. Actual programmes of community care may take many forms, but an important part in any scheme must be played by social workers. The general purposes for which they might be used have been well described by the government's plan for the development of community care:

'A normal person relies on those (with) whom he lives and works for understanding, sympathy and co-opera-tion. Where there is mental disorder these supports may be seriously undermined or even destroyed. The mental health services therefore aim at strengthening them or constructing others in their place. Here the main need is for an effective body of social workers, including mental welfare officers, working closely with General Prac-titioners and hospital staff. By providing a personal service of advice and support for the mentally disordered and for their families, the social worker can do much to prevent a breakdown either of the mentally disordered person or of his social relationships, to obviate the need or re-admission to hospital, or to aid rehabilitation. Through personal contact the social worker can also establish what other services are appropriate and try to ensure that the mentally disordered and their relatives take proper advantage of them.'[1]

This quotation contains the outlines of an ambitious programme, but the main features of the projected services raise many serious difficulties, some of which will now be considered in more detail.

[1] Ministry of Health *Health and welfare: the development of community care* H.M.S.O., 1963. Cmnd. 1973, paragraph 83.

Mental health

(1) *Provision of trained staff.* In an ambitious programme like the one outlined above, an adequate supply of trained staff is clearly vital. The Younghusband Report in 1959 reported that 70 per cent of local authority officers with combined health and welfare duties had no qualifications save experience. It is also estimated that future requirements would be in the nature of 2,000 mental welfare officers and in addition 260 whole-time psychiatric social workers. We are, of course, very far from reaching either of these targets. The Ministry of Health reported in 1962 that the total number of social workers employed by local authorities was 1,247, including '91 psychiatric social workers or others with advanced training'.

Most commentators agree that without the support of a trained social work staff patients and their families will not be able to cope with the strains of living with mental illness in the community. What can be done? More use could be made of part-time workers, and we should do all we can to enable the married woman who has brought up her children to train or re-train for the work. The Samaritans have shown that voluntary work can make a contribution to the solution of social problems. Finally, we should consider the possible redeployment of our existing social workers. It has been argued recently, for example, that psychiatric social workers would work more effectively from a local authority rather than a hospital base where most of them are at present.

(2) *Help to patients and their families.* Local authorities are certainly called upon to provide a large volume of social work service. Returns from local authorities in 1961 showed that a total of 89,687 mentally ill people and just over 11,000 subnormals had been referred from general practitioners, hospitals, police, courts, etc. At the end of that year local authorities were providing some

form of service for over 122,000 cases of mental disorder. It has been estimated that in the next ten years 5 in every 1,000 of the population will require the services of the local authority; and 3 of these will be subnormal.

Each case of mental disorder may involve far more than the patient himself. In a study of just over 4,400 cases[1] the mental health of the patients' nearest relative was rated as disturbed in 60 per cent of the families (in 20 per cent it was rated as severely disturbed). In 35 per cent of the families socil and leisure activities were affected, in 34 per cent children were disturbed and in a quarter of the families income was judged to have been reduced by at least 10 per cent and in one-tenth of the families by more than a half. In addition over one-third of the families found the patient's behaviour he was demanding.

A similar picture of the burdens on families emerges when families with a subnormal member are studied. In nearly half the families in a recent study[2] social contacts were judged to be limited or nearly limited. These families had also carried considerable burdens of anxiety in the past, 37 per cent of the mothers, for instance, had not been told their child was subnormal until after he reached school. As far as present anxieties were concerned only one-third of the women had received medical advice concerning the risks of a further pregnancy. In this and other studies we see a twofold need: for tangible services of help in the home; and for medical and social counselling over emotional problems. It is important if help is to be effective that a drastic divorce should not be allowed to develop between these two services. For instance, Dr Grad, a research worker who had made a

---

[1] J. Grad and P. Sainsbury *Mental illness and the family* in *Lancet* vol. 1., no. 7280. 9th March 1963, p. 544.

[2] J. Tizard and J. Grad *The mentally handicapped and their families* O.U.P., 1961.

significant contribution to the mental health field, stated in a recent lecture that 'it is fashionable to talk about a mother's feeling of guilt at producing an abnormal child rather than her exhaustion at the extra work his prolonged and difficult infancy involves. . . . Nevertheless, the first proposition is speculative and the second known'.[1] Yet the mother's guilt is part of the social worker's knowledge deriving from her fieldwork experience which will enrich her attempts to relieve the physical burdens of the client.

This interelation of practical and emotional factors, which is at the basis of social work, leads us to a second aspect of the family problems of the mentally disordered. This concerns the relationship between the patient and his family. Certainly, some patients come from highly disturbed families, though it is not yet clear how far the disturbance contributes to the onset of the illness or how far it is a reflection of the pressures on the family produced by the illness. Whatever the nature of the family's involvement with its mentally disordered member, research suggests that schizophrenic patients returning from hospital to the care of a relative who shows a high degree of emotional involvement tend to deteriorate more frequently than patients returning to relatives with low emotional involvement.[2]

All these family problems place a heavy burden on the social worker. Often the social worker in the local authority has little or no psychiatric consultation. We talk continually about helping the family as a whole, but we have at present little or no knowledge of how families live together. It has been suggested that in very disturbed

[1] J. Grad *Social work with the families of the mentally subnormal* in Royal Society of Health *Proceedings of the Health Congress* Torquay, 1964.

[2] G. Brown and others *Influence of family life on the course of schizophrenic illness* in British *Journal of Preventive Social Medicine* vol. 16. April 1962, pp. 55–68.

family situations it is 'essential to work with both parents and even the whole family in the reality situation of the here and now, using for one's interpretations the abundant supply of material from the past as well as from the present. This is an attempt to participate as a benevolent, safe, unshockable outsider in the pain, distress and bitterness of the relationships, and yet not to be quite caught up in them. It seems to give the parents strength to see one unshattered, yet not impersonal and detached but warm and human, even humorous, when occasion demands. One tried to catch as much as possible of what is thrown around, showing the family all the while what they are doing and have done to each other, how they misunderstand, misinterpret and so on. . . . Another way of describing one's role is to think of oneself as a receptacle, catching good things and bad things and then acting as a kind of filter so that new insights tend to emerge, different, perhaps less distorted, pictures of the other person, attitudes and qualities which are good and constructive but which had been carelessly discarded. . . . From such a session everyone emerges drained, but with a feeling of satisfaction that something creative has taken place.'[1] This conveys something of the difficult roles a social worker might carry in trying to help some of the disturbed families of the mentally ill.

(3) *Organizational problems.* Many problems in the mental health service revolve around issues of the co-ordination of the three main branches, the General Practitioner, the local authority, and the hospital. Most commentators agree that no branch can successfully operate in isolation. The local authority plans[2] for example, stated that the community care programmes of local authorities are bound up with the future of the

---

[1] E. M. Goldberg *Parents and psychotic sons* in *British Journal of Psychiatric Social Work* vol. 5 no. 4. Autumn 1960, p. 184.

[2] Ministry of Health *Health and welfare, op. cit.*

G.P. service. Similarly, the local authority service cannot be seen as a substitute for that of the hospital: 'home care' cannot stand on its own. If, then, problems of co-ordination are of such importance, what steps have been taken to solve them? A number of authorities have created integrated services. Nottingham, for example, has such a service under the medical officer for mental health who is also superintendent of the local mental hospital: this service is based on the hospital and places considerable emphasis on the part to be played by social workers. Oldham has a combined service based on a psychiatric unit in a general hospital, whilst York's integrated service is based on the appointment of psychiatrists jointly by the hospital and local authority. Other areas provide a district mental health service based exclusively on one branch. The Worthing service of community care, for instance, is provided by the local hospital and has no formal links with the local authority. Finally, many areas rely on the development of a co-operative spirit between workers in the different branches. In Salford, for example, mental welfare officers are assigned their own groups of G.P.'s and are encouraged to make contact with their future clients before they are discharged from the mental hospital.

Conclusion

Whatever the organizational framework in which the social worker in mental health works, he or she clearly carries an important responsibility in executing and modifying our mental health policies. It is part of those responsibilities to try to ensure that equal weight is given to each of the three main branches of the service: the care of the subnormal; of the mentally ill; and of the disturbed child. Administration and procedures must be kept responsive to the needs of those using the services, especially in our present stage of largely experimental work.

The problem of the offender

FRANK DAWTRY

The areas of social work described in previous essays have mostly been concerned with the deprived, the handicapped, the underprivileged and the unfortunate. In general public sympathy is with these people, and with the social worker. The criminal who offends against society's laws, and has been, or is being punished, is far less likely to command public sympathy. When the social worker is asked to step in and help him re-adjust to normal living he may well run up against more resistance and hostility than in other fields.

This situation raises special problems which Frank Dawtry is well equipped to discuss. Secretary since 1948 of the National Association of Probation Officers, he was on the staff of the West Riding Discharged Prisoners' Aid Society from 1927–36, and engaged on prison welfare in Wakefield and Maidstone Prisons from 1937–46. Between 1944–46 he was also Secretary to the National Council for the Abolition of the Death Penalty.

What is an offender? What is he like? The great train robber hits the headlines but the sneak thief does not; the man who commits murder or conducts a massive fraud is tried in a blaze of publicity, but the persistent petty thief may be sentenced in a magistrates' court almost unnoticed. These are all offenders, but they are not all alike. There are offenders who have served their sentences, others on probation or who have been fined, and others who have not been detected, sharing our bus journeys, our cafe meals and our entertainments every day. They have no distinctive marks and are not a race apart.

If the offender, except when committing his offence, is usually indistinguishable from the rest of us, how can he be defined? The widest general definition of the offender is that he is an individual with a defective sense of citizenship – that is, of social responsibility. This does not mean that he may not be responsible for his actions, or that he should not be answerable for them – but whether he robbed a bank or hit an old woman over the head, assaulted a child or committed bigamy, the offender failed in his responsibility to his fellow men and women, whatever the cause or explanation of his conduct. His action was, however, peculiar to himself. Every offender is an individual who at some point has deviated from the normal rules of acceptable conduct, so far as these can be defined by law. He may have been influenced by others or acted with others, but his action is nevertheless his own.

It follows that no generalizations about the treatment of crime can meet the situation revealed by any particular offence or offender. The methods of dealing with offenders must be varied so that the most appropriate can be applied to each individual; and its main purpose should be to help him to improve his defective sense of responsibility if he is capable of doing so. Some offenders pose special problems because they are not able to control their conduct, but the vast majority can be held to account for their behaviour in greater or less degree. Once society has been satisfied that the law has been broken and that the right culprit has been brought to justice, it is entitled to ask why the offender behaved as he did, and to find ways of training or treating him so that he is less likely to offend again and more likely to follow a socially acceptable way of living.

This does not imply that all individuals should be forced into a mould of compliance in the totalitarian manner. On the contrary it means that society, by trying to fit the treatment to the offender, is not disowning him as a citizen, but is accepting its own share of responsibility for him. No man is an island, and any man's failure might be attributable to some extent to a failure on the part of society to meet his needs. His offence may arise from physical, mental or emotional difficulties, in which case these should be treated. His conduct may be due to his own inadequacies which are not obvious until an offence has been committed but which, with skilled help, he can overcome. He may offend because of economic need or because he accepted standards which society has failed to improve. Not every offender, of course, is a sick or sorry specimen, but behind many offences lie often undiscovered explanations, and the number of members of the community who deliberately choose to live by crime and organize their lives for that purpose is very small.

To suggest that the treatment of most offenders should be designed to restore them where possible to socially acceptable living is not to suggest that their offences should be ignored or condoned, but only that condemnation should be combined with measures which will serve the best interest of both the community and the offender by helping the offender to become a law-abiding citizen. Totalitarian methods, brain-washing or simple extermination can of course prevent an individual from returning to crime, but the conception of *helping* him willingly to improve his conduct would seem to be a preferable basis for all treatments. This is no new or revolutionary idea. The Chinese philosopher Lao Tsu wrote 'Only pursue the offender to show him the way'; the Christian doctrine calls for the offender to turn from his wickedness and live; and the principle of regarding the needs of the offender without disregarding the needs of society has been recognized in legislation.

For instance, the Children and Young Persons Act 1933 said that 'every court in dealing with a child or young person . . . shall have regard to the welfare of the child or young person' and the first of the Prison Rules 1964, authorized by the Prison Act 1952, states that 'The purpose of the training and treatment of convicted prisoners shall be to encourage them and assist them to lead a good and useful life' while the Probation of Offenders Act as long ago as 1907 and the Criminal Justice Act 1948 specified the duty of probation officers as being to 'advise, assist and befriend' those put in their care. The law has therefore recognized that the offender may be a person to whose welfare attention should be paid, who shall be befriended, or encouraged to lead a good and useful life.

It would seem desirable for all punishments and treatments available to the courts to embrace those concepts where they can reasonably be applied or seem to be justified.

The vast majority of those dealt with by the courts are of course found guilty of 'non-indictable' offences, which on the whole are the less serious offences, many of them being comparatively minor breaches of the law. Over a million individuals were found guilty of non-indictable offences in England and Wales during 1963. 800,000 of these were involved in traffic offences and 80,000 in offences arising from drunkenness. These may indicate irresponsibility, just as do more serious offences, but they rarely warrant any prolonged treatment, though the very fact of a court appearance and conviction can have a valuable salutary effect. Over 95 per cent of all the non-indictable offenders are fined, and less than 1 per cent of such offenders are sent to prison.

For the more serious offenders more serious penalties are likely to be used. Of all offenders over 21 found guilty of 'indictable' offences, in 1963 (106,116) 23 per cent (24,348) were imprisoned; but of those dealt with in the Assize courts or courts of quarter sessions which deal generally with the most serious matters, 15,813 offenders over the age of 21 were found guilty and 8,910 of these, or 56 per cent were sent to prison. Prison remains as the most severe general sanction in maintaining the law. Can it serve the purpose set out in the Prison Rules?

149

Prison

Imprisonment is a form of banishment from society, for a few days, for months or for years and, apart from capital punishment, it is the harshest expression of the community's disapproval of the offender. Prison was, strangely enough, originally considered to be a humane substitute for more drastic measures. The penal history of this country is a record of violent punishments, torture, whipping and death. Until the early years of last century there were 120 offences for which the penalty could be death, although the actual use of this penalty had diminished as it was replaced by a less drastic form of banishment – transportation. But the idea was the same – that the only thing to do with the offender was to get rid of him. As transportation became difficult for political reasons, and less generally acceptable on humanitarian grounds the use of prison itself as a punishment developed. Prison had originally been only a safe place in which to keep offenders awaiting trial; now it became a penal institution. But the high wall surrounding the prisons built in the nineteenth century was not only intended to prevent the escape of prisoners; it prevented the community's intrusion into prison and thereby perpetuated the separation of the offender from the rest of society. It was almost as effective as the ocean for this purpose. For the majority of prisons the wall remains, today, as the symbol of isolation.

The State thus continues to try what might seem to be the impossible task of educating men and women to live in the community by taking them out of the community into an artificial and abnormal world.

This is not a criticism of those who manage the prisons, or of the prison staff. It is a criticism of an out-of-date system, which has been made worse by overcrowding arising from the increase of convictions in the last ten years. Many prisons are accommodating nearly twice as many prisoners as they were intended to hold; several thousand prisoners have to sleep three in a cell built for one; sanitary conditions remain incredibly archaic, and there is such a shortage of work that many prisoners work as little as eighteen hours a week despite the efforts of the authorities to find more, and more suitable, occupations for them. In such conditions the prison staff have little opportunity to engage in any personal or constructive work with prisoners, and many of them are fully occupied with the task of keeping order and discipline and ensuring that the numbers are correct, morning, noon and night. In such conditions, the good prisoner is the one who obeys all the rules, never takes an individual line, and gets through his sentence with the minimum of trouble for himself and the staff.

The Prison Officers' Association has expressed its opinion that probably less than one in ten of the men in prison is of the vicious, trouble making type who needs to be under conditions of strict security. In a memorandum published in 1964, the Association commented that the average prisoner never has to accept responsibility, usually has insufficient work and that the work available is dull and unimaginative. 'After serving a sentence under these conditions' the officers said 'a man's senses are dulled and he leaves prison knowing only one thing – how to live in prison – so that when he gets out he is less well equipped to face life than when he was sentenced'.

This is hardly the ideal training for citizenship nor does it appear to offer much encouragement to lead a good and useful life. For the weak, inadequate or homeless individual it is not surprising that, despite its limitations, the ease and security of prison is preferable to the uncertainties and responsibilities of the outside world.

It is true of course that during the last forty years, and particularly during and since the last war, efforts have been made to 'break down the wall' by the establishment of open prisons, the use of country houses as penal institutions and the use of prison labour outside prison. In these conditions prisoners have been able to develop responsibility and to carry out a full day's useful work.

Unfortunately the open establishments still accommodate only about 10 per cent of the adult prison population; the other 90 per cent remain behind prison walls. This can hardly be for economic reasons (a poor country like Finland has over 40 per cent of its prisoners in open conditions) for the maintenance of buildings, the staff ratio and other factors are all cheaper for open than for closed institutions, while the work output is higher. Part of the responsibility for the limited use of open methods lies with the community. Every proposal to establish an open institution is met by public protests and delay, and even those members of the public who appreciate the value of open institutions usually consider that they should be located in another part of the country. When an open institution is established, however, it is not uncommon for the local community to participate in its activities and to take pride in doing so.

Closed prisons remain, however, the basis of the penal system. Communal meals, evening activities, allowances of spending money, smoking, free conversation and other reforms have helped to break down the complete monotony of the old prison regime, but these are fringe activities which can do so little to mitigate the effect of prison conditions themselves. Prison visitors and teachers have taken an element of civil life into prison; group discussions and encouragement of staff participation in activities with prisoners; the occasional visits of lecturers and concert parties and the organization of sports and games all represent brave efforts to humanize the system. All this, however, can make little impression on the general effect of prison; nor can it provide much help in dealing with the factors and problems which may in many cases have contributed to the breakdown in the offender's conduct, and to which he must eventually return.

The discharged prisoner

Until recent years, the prisoner's problems have attracted attention only from charitable bodies who have offered limited help and unlimited goodwill to discharged prisoners, but in more recent years state supported central organizations have not only assisted but been responsible for supervising the conduct of certain groups of offenders after discharge. These groups are those released from Borstal, corrective training and preventive detention on a conditional basis and for whom any serious misconduct may lead to a return to the institution to complete their sentences.

Efforts to help the discharged prisoner have usually begun only at the end – or towards the end – of a sentence and they have provided little to counter-balance the effect of imprisonment itself. The prisoner is obviously more likely to succeed on discharge if adequate prior preparation can be made for this. The prison authorities have introduced schemes whereby long sentence prisoners may have the opportunity to spend the last months of their sentences in a hostel attached to the prison, from which they go out to normal employment in the locality and may be allowed to visit friends, a cinema or theatre. This helps to break down the division between prison and the outside world and to accustom the prisoner to a normal day's work. In other cases prisoners nearing the end of a sentence are allowed to visit their homes, see prospective employers and meet those who might help them on discharge. For many, this has served to remove some of their fears about the future.

Such schemes can, however, apply only to a few prisoners, but a serious attempt is now being made to assist prisoners by methods of social work. This has been brought about by the introduction into prisons of social workers who have no part in the discipline of the prison but belong to the outside world. The social worker – the prison welfare officer – is, or should be, free to meet any prisoner, and available to be seen by any prisoner wishing to consult him, or to whose need his attention has been drawn by an official or prison officer. (The prison officer, in daily contact with prisoners, is often in the best position to notice signs of disturbance and difficulty in a prisoner).

The prison welfare officer can offer a prisoner advice and guidance in his personal affairs and social problems in readiness for his discharge, and can get in touch with the prisoner's home or family, or possible employers, either directly or through the agency of social workers (usually a probation officer) in the prisoner's home district. The prisoner can also be helped to gain insight into his own problems and understanding of the part he himself must play in his rehabilitation. On his discharge he will be referred by the welfare officer to the probation and after-care officer (who may, if circumstances permit, have visited him in prison to establish a personal contact) for assistance and support in his efforts to re-establish himself.

The development of this contact between prison welfare officers and probation and after-care officers, each 'speaking the same language' and, it is hoped, in future sharing the same training, may be one of the major steps in the establishment of a comprehensive re-settlement service for ex-prisoners. Hitherto such a service has been limited to a small number of prisoners in specified categories. It is now accepted that the length or type of sentence and the age or experience of the offender do not necessarily provide the best criteria for estimating the need for help on discharge, and the service now being established should make assistance and after-care available to any prisoner according to his need and his ability to respond to the efforts made on his behalf.

This will bring the responsibility for its offenders squarely back onto the shoulders of the community. The ex-prisoner may need lodgings, or a hostel which will not remind him of his prison cell; he may need employment which he can find only if employers are willing to engage ex-prisoners; he will above all need to feel that he is accepted as a normal citizen by the rest of the community. The newly developing plans for a comprehensive after-care service emphasize the part which may be played by voluntary 'auxiliaries'. These will be neither specialists in the treatment of offenders nor well-meaning do-gooders of the patronizing type familiar in Victorian charity. They must be ordinary citizens themselves, ready to behave towards their prisoner friends as they would to any other friends, without embarrassment on either side. They will not be easy to find, but the right sort of volunteers will always be welcomed. Services like those of the Women's Voluntary Service, and those specially concerned with ex-prisoners such as the Blackfriars Settlement in London, the New Bridge, the Simon Community, have shown that carefully selected volunteers can play a vital part in the befriending of prisoners and thus in their reintegration into society.

Is prison necessary?

The unfortunate fact remains that the efforts made on behalf of those leaving prison by welfare officers, probation officers and their voluntary supporters, begin against the background of prison itself; and even the best efforts by the authorities to improve and reform the prisons assume the continued use of imprisonment and the segregation of offenders from the community. It may be time to ask, in the case of many offenders, 'Was their journey (to prison) really necessary?'

Society must, of course, be satisfied that law-breaking

shall not go without control of the offender, and for some offenders punishment is a necessary part of the therapeutic process. Certain offenders must obviously be restrained to prevent the continuance or repetition of their offences, though many of these need treatment rather than restriction. Their restraint can, however, be used as an opportunity for this, and recently the first English prison specializing in the treatment of disturbed prisoners has been opened. Here treatment can be combined with authority and discipline.

Professional criminals such as the planners of bank raids, the fraudulent converters, forgers and others who live by crime must also obviously be kept out of circulation, though they are unlikely to respond to training as they have chosen their careers as others choose more lawful pursuits. For them and for others who constitute a danger to society, institutions must be maintained where they are able to do useful and productive work, which might contribute to the compensation of their victims. Society's best protection against such offenders must nevertheless be provided by more adequate preventive and detective forces.

The highly organized, deliberate and more serious offenders form a very small proportion of the prison population. Of the convicted offenders sent to prison or other penal institutions today, about 70 per cent serve sentences of six months or less, and over half are sentenced to three months or less. It is idle to pretend that these sentences can provide any opportunity for the training and treatment referred to in the Prison Rules. Many of the men and women serving these sentences will have been to prison before, perhaps many times. They have obviously not gained much benefit from earlier sentences, yet these are repeated. Others will be serving their first sentences and while they will find the experience degrading it will provide them only with the ability to tolerate prison. For the majority of prisoners, whatever may be considered to be their deserts, prison amounts to little more than a waste of time. It is also a waste of time for prison officers and staff, and a waste of money. It costs an average of over £500 per year to keep a prisoner in prison, while his family may have to be maintained from public funds, and his employment may be disrupted or lost. Prison welfare officers and after-care agencies will do their best to help, but this help could usually be given more directly and practically if the offender were to remain free in the community; prison may hinder the process and make assistance more difficult.

Despite this, new closed and cellular prisons are being built, at very high cost. They are no doubt intended to replace the oldest and most objectionable prisons whenever the crime situation allows any of these to be closed, but they perpetuate the belief in the value of imprisonment when this must be seriously questioned.

The alternatives

As has been shown, even in the case of serious offenders imprisonment is now used only to a limited extent, and for the less serious offences it is hardly used at all.

However, if the use of prison should be further restricted, what are the alternatives? The most common, already in use, is the imposition of a fine. Even for indictable offences in 1963, more than 85,000 were dealt with by fining.

Fining, of course, rarely serves any constructive purpose. The other most widely used and more constructive alternative is probation. While there are less than 30,000 convicted offenders in prisons and other penal institutions today, there are over 75,000 convicted offenders on probation. Many of these are children and young persons, but of convicted offenders over the age of 21 there were (in 1963) just over 24,000 in prison on any one day, and about 22,500 on probation. The latter

157

are by no means all first offenders or perpetrators of less serious crimes; the Judges and Recorders, who deal with the more serious and persistent offenders, in 1963 placed 2,299 offenders over the age of 21 on probation; the magistrate, dealing with the same age group of indictable offenders, placed over 9,000 on probation (and fined over 50,000). There is obviously a considerable element of chance about the treatment of offenders – yet, at least for first offenders, it has been shown that they are equally likely to remain out of further trouble whether they are fined, placed on probation or sent to prison.

Probation has shown that many offenders can quite reasonably and safely remain in the community. The disapproval of their conduct is demonstrated by the conviction for an offence, but the offender is dealt with as a person capable of responding to treatment or advice. By placing him on probation the court offers him the opportunity to behave more responsibly and shares that responsibility with him by placing him under the supervision of a probation officer. The officer will keep in touch with him both at home and at the probation office, assist him in any way which seems necessary and possible, and provide guidance and advice in the direction of his affairs and the sorting out of his problems. These may be personal, or personality, problems or matters of relationship with parents, wife, neighbours or employers, and the offender can often be helped to understand his own part in the improvement of these relationships. He may be a seriously disturbed individual needing the help of a doctor or psychiatrist in which case the probation officer will try to arrange for this, and encourage the probationer to accept it (though there are grave shortages of clinics and psychiatrists for this purpose). The offender may need lodgings, or work, or wish to make a fresh start in a new district, and efforts will be made to help him in such matters.

While this goes on with and for the offender, the

probation officer retains the authority given to him by he court to supervise the conduct and habits of the offender, and if the probationer refuses to co-operate with the probation officer he can be taken back to the court which placed him on probation, and that court can terminate the probation order and substitute a more drastic penalty for the offence for which the probation order was made. What is more, if a person commits a further offence while on probation he may be sentenced for that offence and additionally for the original offence for which he was placed on probation. Probation is not, therefore, a 'let-off', but a controlled effort to protect the public while at the same time assisting the offender to become a better citizen.

There are failures and disappointments in probation as in all treatments and some failure is inherent in the system – for probation used only where it was certain to succeed would in fact be used in many cases where it was not necessary. Like all services dealing with offenders, the probation service is seriously short of officers, who have an average of fifty to sixty cases each on their lists so that the chance of giving sufficient individual attention and advice, assistance and friendship to each of their cases is very slender. Probation officers are also called upon to make reports for the assistance of the courts and to carry out many other duties in the field of matrimonial conciliation, adoption proceedings and the supervision of young people considered to be in need of care, protection or control, in addition to the provision of after-care for offenders returning from prison and other penal institutions.

With the offender placed on probation the officer will try gradually to establish a relationship in which help and mutual understanding will become possible. But the man coming from prison is faced with a sudden change from the shelter of prison to the responsibilities of civilian life and his needs may be immediate and urgent, while he may carry with him resentment about his imprisonment and an objection to any representative of authority. Though probation and after-care differ, therefore, in the intensity of the problems they involve, both call for the same basic social skills; the treatment of the offender in the open, whether on probation or after punishment, must depend upon personal relationships of confidence being built up between the offender and those working with him. The development of these depends primarily on the quality of the individuals attempting to establish them. Just as a bad prison officer can pollute a prison, so an ineffective probation officer can do more harm than good, and a high degree of training and skill is called for in all who undertake this work.

Other treatments

Between the absolute freedom of the offender who has been fined or discharged by the court (which often happens in the case of trivial offences), the controlled freedom of probation, and the restrictive conditions of prison, other alternative treatments are available. For young offenders, Borstal and detention centres provide modified forms of training in custody, and approved schools combine continued education with training and discipline. In both borstal and approved schools industrial training can give an opportunity for inmates to learn the basic skills of a trade.

The attendance centre, which a young offender may be ordered to attend on Saturday afternoons over a period, has provided a minor but useful control over conduct. It interferes with leisure activities and provides an opportunity for physical training and other pursuits under strict discipline. One centre for youths in the 18–21 age group has proved very successful and the use of such centres (perhaps open in the evenings) which older offenders could be compelled to attend would seem to offer a cheap and non-disruptive method of treatment which could include learning of domestic crafts.

For offenders under the age of 21, probation may be combined with a requirement to reside for a period of up to twelve months in a probation home or hostel. In a home the probationers live and work together under the guidance of the warden; in a hostel, they live in conditions as near to a normal family life as possible, go out to work in local industries, pay for their maintenance, are allowed pocket money, and are under the guidance and supervision of the warden. In some cases a home or hostel enables a young probationer to be kept away from a bad home or environment, while the probation officer in his home area attempts to improve home conditions and advise the parents. A period of residence in a home or hostel is usually followed by a further period under the supervision of the probation officer.

The use of probation homes and hostels has set a pattern which many believe could be extended to older offenders. For those not on probation, similar provisions have already demonstrated their worth. Norman House in North London was established to accommodate homeless ex-prisoners, many of whom were incapable of ordering their own lives. With the security of a home and constant personal support, many have been helped to take and keep employment and eventually to move into private lodgings and make their own way in the world. Some have failed but many succeeded and the value of this 'half-way house' between the shelter of prison and the bleak realities of the outside world has encouraged a number of religious organizations and other bodies to establish similar hostels. This development suggests that hostels could be used for many now coming to them, but without the necessity of first going to prison. Residence in such hostels combined with a measure of supervision might help some, who now drift in and out of prison, to avoid prison altogether.

Prevention

There is an urgent need for more research into these and other methods for dealing with offenders, and more study by the courts of the existing methods so that they might be used in the manner most appropriate for any offender.

Unfortunately, treatment of offenders can usually start only when an offence has been committed, but for young people the Children and Young Persons Act 1963 gave local authorities, through their children's services, the opportunity to intervene, and to provide support and help, where conditions seemed likely to lead to the appearance of a child or young person in court. It also provided for the establishment of family advice services for the guidance of parents in difficulties over family problems. Police liaison services in a number of areas also provide guidance and advice as a substitute for a court appearance, for young first offenders.

These constructive services are already reducing the numbers of children appearing before the juvenile courts (apart from the effect of raising the age of criminal responsibility) and the growth of preventive services is eminently desirable. There may be dangers, however, if officials are provided with power to deprive any individual of his liberty, even for apparently socially desirable reasons. Such deprivation of liberty must remain a matter for the courts, who can call upon the children's service, probation service, mental health or hospital services if they are satisfied about the need for treatment or guidance from any of these.

Acting on information

Every decision by a court should, however, be based on adequate knowledge of the offender and his circumstances. Many courts still work in the dark, or allow themselves to be affected by their reactions to a particular offence or offender regardless of his real need.

The problem of the offender

Some are too lenient, while in others offenders are sometimes treated briefly and brusquely by a court anxious to satisfy public opinion that crime is being dealt with. If the treatment is the wrong one, however, the offender may merely be hardened in his ways, or encouraged in his wrongdoing. It is desirable that any court, after satisfying itself about the facts of the situation, should have available information to enable it to assess the offender and find the most appropriate combination of punishment and treatment. This need is met by the use of 'social enquiry reports' which are in most cases prepared by probation officers whose experience gives them the ability to assess characters and motives and discover factors which may have influenced an offender's conduct. Juvenile courts are obliged to obtain a social enquiry report on every child or young person coming before them for anything but a trivial offence, but in the magistrates' courts and higher courts (except when they are considering the imprisonment of a first offender) such reports are only supplied when asked for by the court. The Streatfeild Committee (1961) emphasized the importance of such reports, because 'where the court is seeking to reform, to deter or to protect, it is seeking to control future events rather than simply to pass judgment on past events'. This Committee's recommendations have led to very extensive use of reports in the higher courts and it is equally desirable that the magistrates' courts also should be provided with them, so that the treatment of every offender may be decided upon only in the light of the fullest possible information.

* * *

The paramount need in dealing with offenders is that, in the first place there should be adequate preventive, diagnostic and treatment services so that, so far as this can be assured by human judgment, the treatment of any offender should be the most suitable one for him, though this may lead to sentences which do not appear to match, or be justified by, the offence. The second need is that the community shall be willing to accept responsibility for the rehabilitation of offenders, whether they remain in society or return to society after a period spent in an institution. This can be done by the provision of much strengthened child-care, probation and after-care services, supported by voluntary effort, hostels for the homeless and inadequate, and a willingness to regard offenders as usually normal, but temporarily deviant, citizens. Above all, it is necessary for the community to share the belief, expressed by the late Archbishop Temple, that no man is a criminal and nothing else.

The voluntary contribution

DAVID HOBMAN

The importance of voluntary organizations and voluntary workers in social welfare is immense. Some services, especially those for old people, could hardly operate without their contribution.

David Hobman is the Information Officer of the National Council of Social Service. He was formerly a Regional Officer in Eastern England, has been Secretary of the Cumberland Council of Social Service, Warden of a Community Centre, a Youth Club Leader and in 1957 worked with the Hungarian Division of the British Council for Aid to Refugees. He also acts as Information Officer to the Standing Conference of Organizations of Social Workers, and is a visiting lecturer at the National Institute for Social Work Training.

A frequent lecturer and broadcaster on social welfare, he is the author of *A guide to voluntary service* (1964) and a pamphlet *Leisure and pleasure* (1965).

Throughout history voluntary enterprise has represented an important aspect of British social life. Between them, the volunteers of past ages pioneered the majority of services now administered by the State, and largely taken for granted as part of the normal fabric of social life. By the beginning of the present century there was growing acceptance of the fact that much of the pioneer work undertaken by voluntary societies ought to be integrated with the services of the State. This was acknowledged by the members of the 1909 Poor Law Commission who said in their Majority Report 'We are convinced, and the evidence has, in our opinion, amply shown, that the charities should be brought into the field of public work and responsibility, and that, expressly or tacitly, obligations should be imposed upon them which are consistent with the purpose for which they were established'.[1] The Minority Report, also expressed some concern about the effect of indiscriminate charity. 'With regard to the whole range of charitable work in connection with the home life of the poor, there is, in our judgment, nothing more disastrous . . . than the alms dispensed by well-meaning persons in the relief of distress.'

But the authors of the Majority Report also said 'We think it should be the cardinal principle of public administration that the utmost use should under proper conditions, be made of voluntary agencies and of the personal service of men and women of goodwill. But it is, in our opinion, essential that the proper sphere of this voluntary effort should be clearly understood'. Such a view would be generally acceptable today.

The pattern of growth

An indication of the pattern of the growth of voluntary organizations can be seen in the introduction to a handbook published by the National Council of Social Service entitled *Voluntary social services*.[2] It contains a chart of the number established in various periods since the latter half of the seventeenth century as follows:

Period	Organizations
1650–99	3
1800–49	13
1850–79	31
1880–89	18
1890–99	16
1900–09	16
1910–19	37
1920–29	36

[1] Royal Commission on the Poor Law and Relief of Distress *Report* 1909.

[2] National Council of Social Service *Voluntary social services* 6th edn. 1964.

1930–39	47
1940–49	53
1950–59	28

The chart reveals the substantial growth recorded during the period covered by the last war, and the years immediately afterwards when the Welfare State was being evolved; this largely disproves the view expressed by those who felt there would be no further need for voluntary action within a comprehensive system of social security.

Although the chart illustrates the widespread development of voluntary organizations during the twentieth century, it does not indicate the actual growth in their membership or the extension of their functions; nor does it take into account the increasing number of amalgamations that have taken place between societies having somewhat similar purposes, which have come together in a unified constitution or in general federation. One definition of a 'voluntary organization' describes it as 'a body which determines its own policy, which relies in some measure for its income upon voluntary sources, and which is likely to employ some unpaid workers in carrying out its functions'.[1]

But increasingly the functions of voluntary organizations have become more complex. For example, in a number of specialized fields voluntary organizations may be largely staffed by trained, paid social workers and administrators (for example, the Family Welfare Association).

Conversely, statutory authorities may augment their personnel with volunteers in meeting certain of their responsibilities. In this situation planned co-operation and mergers are common. The creation of the Spastics Society, for example, brought together in 1962 two organizations with similar objectives: the British Council

[1] Madeline Rooff *Voluntary societies and social policy* Routledge, 1957.

for the Welfare of Spastics and the National Spastics Society. An example of the need for co-operation of another kind which leads to joint action in a less formal setting, is to be found in the creation of the National Bureau for Co-operation in Child Care established in 1963. This came about because leaders of professional and voluntary agencies in the many social and medical disciplines involved in the total operation of child care felt the need for an effective system of communications as their individual specialization increased and the technical language developed by one profession became increasingly incomprehensible to the others.

The idea of partnership between public and voluntary bodies is not new, as the Poor Law Commission had suggested over fifty years ago. Lord Beveridge pointed out in his book *Voluntary action*,[1] written just after the second world war, that 'co-operation between public and voluntary agencies . . is one of the special features of British public life'. The government Report on Charitable Trusts published in 1952, which arose out of Beveridge's book, expressed similar views suggesting that 'State action and voluntary action were not the antithesis of each other; rather they sprang from the same roots, were designed to meet the same needs and had the same motivating forces behind them – indeed State action is voluntary action crystallized and made universal'.[2]

The difference between the situation in 1952 and that of 1909 was that co-operation and co-ordination now represented common practice rather than a general theory occasionally applied. The machinery for co-ordination between voluntary organizations and public authorities developed by the National Council of Social Service and

---

[1] Lord Beveridge *Voluntary action: a report on methods of social advance* Allen & Unwin, 1948.

[2] Prime Minister's Office *Report of the Committee on the Law and Practice Relating to Charitable Trusts* (Nathan Committee) H.M.S.O., 1952. Cmnd. 8710.

its local counterparts throughout the country had been proved to be both feasible and relevant to modern trends.

Councils of social service

The council of social service movement stemmed from the founding of the Charity Organization Society (now the Family Welfare Association) in 1869. The Society introduced the concept of co-operation by establishing a mutual register of cases for those who were administering charitable support to the social casualties of the industrial revolution. Its purpose was to secure the most effective deployment of resources by seeking to avoid the inevitable duplication and gaps in the random dispensation of aid based upon a number of isolated and unrelated schemes.

Citizens' advice bureaux

Another product of the family case work agencies was the citizen's advice bureau movement,[1] which developed the system of an advice and information service from a war-time measure in 1939, to one of the greatest voluntary enterprises of the present day, now annually dealing with over a million enquiries, and which depends substantially upon the services of volunteers for its fulfilment.

The citizens' advice bureaux provide an excellent example of a service which it might be thought could be equally well provided by the staff of public authorities as by the volunteers attached to independent agencies linked through a central service and led where necessary by full-time paid organizers. A number of local authorities do provide information services and they are clearly perfectly well able to do so competently. However, it has been found that the C.A.B. service operates most effectively in a voluntary setting because the public prefers to seek information from an independent but

[1] National Council of Social Service. *The story of the Citizens' Advice Bureaux* 1964.

reliable source, particularly as in many cases the questions asked relate to some form of conflict with authority in one of its guises – the State, landlord, employer.

Official documents are often almost impossible to understand and therefore difficult to accept by the layman, for whom the C.A.B. worker acts as an 'interpreter'. There is also the curious situation that as more sources of aid and protection become available to the public, the less likely the average citizen will know how and where to make use of them. The C.A.B. therefore serves as a direction finder. Another of its functions is to act as a catalyst and relate similar problems being exposed throughout the country, in order to provide an authentic 'social barometer'.

The fact that the C.A.B. service can actually enhance the process of government, by providing a link between the legislative and the individual, is recognized by the grant aid given to the National C.A.B. Council by the Ministry of Housing and Local Government, and the Board of Trade (for its specialized work in consumer advice) and is why the great majority of local bureaux throughout the country are supported by their respective local authorities under provisions contained in the Local Government Act of 1948.

Grant aid

This power to support voluntary societies is now widespread. Apart from the Local Government Act, 1948, many other Acts contain provisions under which local authorities can support the work of voluntary societies working in the various welfare and educational fields specified. (The Physical Training and Recreation Act, 1937; the Education Act, 1944; the National Health Service Act, 1946; the National Assistance Act, 1948; the Housing Act, 1957; and the London Government Act, 1963). In order to maintain its independence of action it is clearly advisable for a voluntary organization to raise at least a proportion of its funds from voluntary sources. But it is equally clear that if the quality of life of a community can be enhanced by the personal service of volunteers, it is better they should be provided with the basic materials, and should not have to spend a great deal of time in fund-raising activities which means that the actual work to be undertaken is reduced in scope.

However each decision about grant aid has to be taken separately, and public authorities have a responsibility to allocate the funds entrusted to them from the public purse carefully. All the same, there are still too many instances when the argument presented, both by the voluntary agencies themselves, and within the Council Chamber, suggests that the criteria for giving support rests upon the voluntary organizations capacity to undertake the work at a lower cost. This may be a factor, but expediency and economy are no substitute for effectiveness, and the inherent virtue in a particular operation being undertaken by volunteers.

In many cases voluntary action will represent an extension of the public authorities' own programmes, as in the case of the delivery of meals on wheels for the housebound, or in the development of housing associations to relieve a situation which is still universally acute. In addition, support to voluntary agencies often provides the means of allowing the ultimate beneficiaries to take a full part in establishing and running the services themselves and, therefore, of ensuring that they are what are actually required.

Co-ordinated action

The process of joint action, 'community organization', in which public resources and voluntary enterprise are linked, has been practised for many years by councils of social service and other similar groupings.

Perhaps the most far-reaching and effective pattern is to be seen in the field of old people's welfare. Here there is now a network of over 1,500 local committees linked together with the National Old People's Welfare Council. They have a two-fold responsibility. Firstly, to provide a forum for discussion, and a focus for the work of the many organizations involved. Secondly, the old peoples' welfare committees can secure general agreement about the best means of achieving a particular objective through existing resources or can take direct action as the corporate expression of the voluntary movement by introducing new services, and if necessary by creating an organization for a particular purpose – for instance, a housing association, sheltered workshop or club. The welfare committees also provide the link between the voluntary movement as a whole, and the various local authority and central government departments having responsibility for providing services for the elderly.

Co-ordinated action is increasingly accepted as the practical means of achieving common objectives, but because voluntary societies have always depended upon the single-minded and dedicated action of their members, this has sometimes led to difficulties in seeing wider perspectives and of the ultimate wisdom of pooling resources.

The representatives of several organizations which provided clubs for the handicapped in a large provincial town recently came to the conclusion that they each required the limited service of a purpose-built ambulance van in order to transport members to their weekly sessions. None of the societies involved required the exclusive use of the vehicle, nor were they each likely to be able to raise sufficient money in a reasonably short time to purchase one. They therefore decided to combine in establishing a council of social service. In the process of coming together it was discovered that there were hitherto unknown sources of help available in the town, which had not previously been mobilized. As a result, the first decision taken by the council of social service, in the light of this new knowledge was that the offers of help and transport made the purchase of a van unnecessary. They then looked at other needs, and embarked upon a number of projects which had earlier been neglected, but which were now seen to be both necessary and possible.

Perhaps the most significant development in co-operation in recent years was suggested by the series of circulars prepared by the Ministry of Health from 1962 onwards,[1] in connection with the Ten Year Plans which the local health and welfare authorities and hospital boards were being asked to prepare as a long term assessment of the demands likely to be made upon them, and of their proposals for meeting them, within a policy of community care.

Planning for expansion

Before the circulars from the Ministry were despatched a series of conferences were held between the Minister and his advisers with representatives of the major national voluntary agencies active in the field. Here it was agreed there was scope for considerable expansion of voluntary effort; that the spread of the work was uneven, but where it was being satisfactorily undertaken it was not to be disturbed. The circulars went on to stress the importance of regular consultation in successful co-operation, and the authorities were asked to consider the scope and effectiveness of the machinery for consultation in their areas. Where it did not already exist (i.e. through councils of social service, old people's welfare committees, etc.), they were asked that steps should be taken to create it.

Each of the circulars contained an appendix setting out a list of the services already provided from which it can be seen that the total contribution of volunteers should not be underestimated. The withdrawal of this

[1] Ministry of Health *Health and welfare op. cit.*

source of help would have serious repercussions and could not be easily replaced. The tasks shown to be undertaken range from those which require little skill and no training to those for which selection and training are demanded (see Appendix III).

Voluntary and professional workers

An analysis of the Appendix reveals two important common denominators which link the majority of the tasks. They involve sustained and regular personal service, and they are integral parts of the administration, which means that the volunteers are required to work in close harmony with professional workers. It is, therefore, of the utmost importance that satisfactory relationships should be established. Volunteers need to know that hard pressed social workers will not resist offers of help. For their part, social workers need to know that volunteers will respond in a disciplined way and will be as aware of their limitations as of their good intentions.

When harmonious relationships are established, the help of the volunteer can be seen as an effective extension to services which are now, and are likely to remain, under severe pressure. As a result, new patterns of co-operation are already emerging in a number of fields, particularly in probation, mental health and after-care.

After-care services is a good example of this general trend towards auxiliary help. For more than a century the welfare of discharged prisoners remained chiefly in the hands of voluntary organizations, with the minimum of salaried staff supervising the work of unpaid helpers. In 1963 the Report of the Home Secretary's Advisory Council on the Treatment of Offenders[1] recommended the ending of this system and said that responsibility for the care of persons discharged from all forms of penal and reformative custody should be in the hands of

[1] Home Office *The organisation of after-care*; report of the Advisory Council on the Treatment of Offenders H.M.S.O., 1963.

an enlarged probation and after-care service. It was generally accepted that only a national service with substantial resources could deal effectively with a major social problem of this nature and magnitude. However, the Advisory Council's Report went on to say 'When the Probation and After-Care Service is established there will still be an indispensable part to be played by voluntary workers as auxiliaries to probation and after-care officers. The main need of many offenders is for simple encouragement, friendship and human understanding which could be given by sincere and warmhearted auxiliaries who had sound commonsense and the ability to make themselves acceptable to those whom they sought to help'. Later on, the Report discusses the need for training. It says 'It is necessary to stress that this is not work for inexperienced amateurs. It requires a warm heart but also a clear head, compassion combined with insight, lack of illusion, and preparedness for disappointment ... most auxiliaries will find their good intentions more effectively translated into rewarding achievement if they can have some training and can work under the regular guidance of professional social workers'.

Training

Training is therefore one of the keys to voluntary service, and it probably represents the major change of recent years. This is because it represents a new *attitude*, which should not be confused with *motive*. Man's motives for social work – whether paid or voluntary – have probably represented a mixture of differing emotions and responses, and it is likely that they always will. But present day volunteers are increasingly prepared to submit themselves to a thorough process of selection and training, if it can be established that the effectiveness of the work demands this. A growing number of voluntary agencies are introducing training programmes in connection with special aspects of their work. Systems of selection and training have long been used by the British Red Cross Society which has prepared a *Welfare services manual* for its volunteers comparable in standard to those used for many years in the fields of first aid and home nursing, where successful completion leads to the award of a recognized certificate.

The work of Marriage Guidance Councils and Citizens' Advice Bureaux is substantially dependent upon the attitude and careful preparation of volunteers, where mere good intentions are not sufficient. The Marriage Guidance Counsellor must, first of all, be happily married and fall within a prescribed age range. After local nominations have been made and interviews have taken place a more intensive process of selection follows during a series of residential weekends supervised by experienced councillors, doctors, psychologists and others qualified to assess the candidates temperamental suitability and aptitudes. About 50 per cent of those who volunteer are likely to be rejected; although this should not be taken to mean they are not well equipped to undertake some less exacting and intensely personal form of service.

Citizens' Advice Bureaux workers are asked to submit the names of people who can act as referees, and also go through a process of selection and training which is concentrated in its initial stages on a carefully planned series of lectures. This is continued by means of regular consultations and conferences, arranged to provide information about new legislation and questions likely to be encountered in the everyday work of the bureaux.

In other organizations training in a formal setting may be introduced at a later stage. For instance, in the w.v.s., members are first recruited to undertake tasks which they can do without preparation. Training is introduced later, for those who are to undertake tasks of special responsibility. The National Old Peoples' Welfare Council arranges training at local regional and national level and to date some 17,000 people have attended one or other of its courses.

A recent development in training can be seen in the increasing number of general introductory courses run by councils of social service and similar bodies, in co-operation with university extra-mural boards and local education authorities. The correspondence course run by the National Extension College conjointly with the present BBC Television series is a further example. All these are designed to give the uncommitted a general background to the social services and the areas of work in which volunteers are active, in order to help them identify their interest and to discover how their particular skills can best be applied; although voluntary service relies basically upon a mixture of common sense and good nature, there are situations where special talents and academic qualifications can be applied.

Opportunities in voluntary work

Changing social conditions, more leisure and earlier retirement have resulted in increased opportunities for community service, and there must be many people who have considered offering their services, but who have hesitated simply through lack of knowledge of the actual opportunities available. In order to provide general information the government published in 1964 *A guide to voluntary service*.[1] This booklet suggests ways in which information can be obtained and first steps taken. It then divides voluntary work under a number of main headings – children, the family, the elderly, and so on, and illustrates the work being undertaken in each of these areas. In a number of places local directories are also published listing the actual work in greater detail. The following illustration from the booklet prepared by the London Council of Social Service, *Some opportunities*

[1] Treasury *A guide to voluntary service*; by D. Hobman H.M.S.O., 1964

The social workers

for voluntary service in London[1] are selected at random from a list of upwards of a hundred Societies:

Invalid Children's Aid Association

Voluntary work: case work, clerical work and appeals functions, driving children.

Qualifications: social work training, shorthand and typing, or knowledge of accounts.

Hours: 9.30 a.m.–5.30 p.m. Expenses paid in some circumstances.

Women's Voluntary Service for Civil Defence

Undertakes a wide variety of services to all sections of the community. Local offices in almost every borough in London area.

Voluntary work: administrative; clerical; driving vans and cars; meals on wheels and luncheon clubs; escort work; visiting old people, problem families, etc.; trolley shops, canteens, etc., in hospitals; children's welfare; Civil Defence; distributing clothing; welfare work with Servicemen overseas, and welfare work for disabled people.

Qualifications: overseas welfare workers must be between 25 and 40 and have had previous experience of welfare work, and experience in organizing social activities.

Hours: week-days (full or part-time), evenings and week-ends.

London Marriage Guidance Council

Voluntary work: marriage counselling, group leadership.

Qualifications: married men or women of understanding and integrity, preferably aged 30 to 50 who are neither divorced nor separated and who accept the principles and aims of the movement.

Selection and training carried out by the National Marriage Guidance Council.

Hours: about six hours a week. Expenses paid.

[1] London Council of Social Service *Some opportunities for voluntary social service in London* 1962.

The voluntary contribution

British Red Cross Society

Voluntary work: help in clinics, hospitals and first-aid posts, help in divisional offices, help with welfare sections at clubs for disabled or aged, help with lunch clubs and meals on wheels, visiting, driving, interpreting, handicraft instruction, help with cadets.

Qualifications: workers in hospitals and first-aid posts need first-aid and home nursing certificates. Typing useful for office work. Selection by interview.

Hours: 9.30 a.m.–5.30 p.m. (certain welfare duties on Saturdays and weekends).

Expenses arranged with individual.

However, in spite of all the efforts to attract people's attention to the needs of the community a great deal more will have to be achieved in the way of recruitment before needs are fully met, and new approaches may be necessary. Experiments are already being undertaken in several areas with the provision of a general information service which can direct the enquiring volunteer towards a Society where his services may be most urgently required at a given time, but these are still limited in number. But co-operation of this kind depends upon agreement about general objectives and priorities; and willingness to pool resources and spend less time in counting heads than has sometimes been the case in the past.

The future

The voluntary movement's responsibility is by no means restricted to personal service. It still has important functions to perform in stimulating research, in educating the public about major social issues, and in the creation and use of amenities. It has already given an effective lead in the provision of overseas aid and relief. It can mobilize public opinion about what are seen to be widespread needs or shortcomings in the system. In order to

179

achieve these general aims it needs to be well organized, often on a national basis, but its effectiveness ultimately lies in the many local variations of method and structure.

Finally, another passage from the Report on Charitable Trusts sums up the process, the people, and the place of voluntary service: 'Not only does voluntary service act as a nursery for the democracy, but also as the field in which good neighbourliness may be exercised. Many tributes have been paid to the voluntary worker but fewer to the good neighbour. Yet in an urban society like ours, too prone to become "a disordered dust of individuals" it is the informal unorganized actions of the good neighbour which make satisfactory relationships possible. We think of a family which invites the lonely worker in a strange new town to Sunday supper, which takes into its home a child whose mother has to go into hospital, which helps an old pensioner with the shopping, which minds a baby so that the young married couple can go out together, which helps rather than ostracizes the sub-standard family. Traditionally it is the churches who have been most active in such forms of good neighbourliness. Fortunately the impulse is wider than the bounds of formal religion, for there has never been greater need than in our own day for the spirit of good neighbourliness among the people at large. More leisure and a better standard of living have provided opportunities of voluntary service to the many which were before only available to the comparatively few. It is therefore essential that such voluntary action in the form of good neighbourliness, voluntary service and financial support should come to be regarded as a normal part of citizenship in the modern democratic state.'[1]

[1] *Report . . . on Charitable Trusts op. cit.*

Postscript

DAME EILEEN YOUNGHUSBAND

The essays in this book, although covering different specialisms in social welfare, have raised a large number of points common to the whole field of social work. More and more social workers are recognizing their essential relationship with each other and the common basis of their work.

In this postscript Dame Eileen Younghusband adds a personal note on problems, solutions and future developments. Currently a consultant on social work training at the National Institute for Social Work Training, Chairman of the Hammersmith Juvenile Court, President of the International Association of Schools of Social Work she is an outstanding figure in the field today. Her publications include *Social work in Britain* (1952), *Third international survey of training for social work* (1959), and *Social work and social change* (1964).

The term 'social work' is often used to cover three separate things – social need, social agencies (or services) and social work. The first term, social need, refers to people who because of their own personalities or a breakdown in their family relationships or because of their social and economic circumstances are not able to cope with life without external help. This help may come from friends or neighbours or it may be met by public or voluntary social services. These services are the second element in the trilogy. In modern society an elaborate organizational, administrative and legal structure is necessary to meet social need and regulate social living. This is provided through both goods and services. But there are some needs that can only be met by an individual professional service. This is the key point at which social needs, social agencies and social work come together. Social work is the profession par excellence

181

concerned with meeting those particular social needs which are centred in people's inability to cope with their personal/social problems. This may happen because the odds are too heavily weighted against them, or because they are immature or inadequate or at loggerheads with society or faced with a sudden crisis which disrupts their normal ability to manage their affairs.

Provision for this particular kind of help to those in personal/social need is scattered piecemeal throughout our social services, with many gaps and some over-lapping. For several years now there has been talk about the need for a comprehensive family service, a service that would provide for social well-being, protection and care. At the moment such a service is only at the talk and thought stage. Maybe the next stage is a government committee of enquiry, coupled with legislation to intro-duce a limited family service as a first step to a 'social' service as comprehensive as the present health and education services. In the meantime, some local author-ities are experimenting with the family advice centres recommended by the Ingleby Report. Some of those who come will require skilled and perhaps prolonged case-work and other service, for others factual information or the kind of advice that puts two and two together will be enough.

In the beginning these family advice centres will be feel-ing their way. They will not always be adequately staffed either in terms of numbers or skill. They will also be experimental because we do not know the range of need and problems that will come to them as people become aware of their existence; nor do we know whether existing services will be sufficient to provide all that is required. It seems simple common sense to conclude that this will be more adequate in some parts of the country than others.

Various enquiries have thrown new light on the extreme stress – personal, social and economic – to which single parent families are subject, where the mother is unmarried or either parent is deserted, divorced, or dead. This concern is of course related to the studies – primarily associated with the name of Dr John Bowlby – which show how vital is the continuing care of one adult for the well-being and future mental health of young children. This is leading not only to new thought about the supporting service – and the sheer support – needed by single parent families, but also to fresh concern about what is happening to the highly vulnerable child under five. Many such children are in high flats with no real play space, or in the often unsuitable care of child minders, or in other circumstances in which they do not receive either the mental stimulus or the emotional and social nurture without which they are likely to grow up into stunted people.

It is very fashionable to talk about prevention, especially since children's departments were required under the 1963 Children and Young Persons Act to prevent the need to receive children into care. But prevention is many sided and not so simple as it may sound. It obviously includes intervention at an early stage in individual crises and also steps to prevent the danger from ever arising. The first type calls for early detection and suitable action, neither by any means simple in practice. The second is still more complex because in a rapidly changing society it can only mean conscious planning of the social environment so as to promote positive mental health and a strong network of social relationships. So far, we only have the most rudimentary conception of how this might be done.

Another blessed term at the present day is community care. This concept has naturally evolved from an earlier swing away from residential care, whether in children's homes, hospitals, prison, old people's homes or mental hospitals. In some instances people were kept in institutions long after they could have lived independently –

and sometimes they became too institutionalized to do so. Or else they went into institutions when they could have been treated at home if better resources had been available. This has led to a good deal more interest in various alternatives as, for example, becoming an accepted member of another family. This is called foster home placement if it refers to children but the same essential device is also being used for old people, the mentally disordered, ex-prisoners and young delinquents. Another admirable device is the hostel which provides some degree of sheltered living, control and protection from which residents go out to work. The same general pattern of semi-supervised living applies also to day hospitals, social centres, sheltered workshops, and clubs. It is a device which could probably be more widely extended. Then there are the domiciliary services of nursing, home helps, health visitors, home teachers and social workers for people who are able to live at home if services are provided and the strain on them and their families is lessened. This also includes practical measures like meals on wheels, aids to mobility, adaptions to the house for handicapped people, and so forth.

But community care is wider than this. It not only includes public and voluntary services, but – equally important – the family which is willing to have an ex-prisoner as a lodger, and also workmates and employers prepared to accept him. It relies upon neighbours who do not shun the spastic in his wheelchair nor the deaf old lady; and people who are willing not only to do the little extras once or twice but also to give longstanding friendship to the isolated and the odd man out. Without this, community care can be worse, more lonely, than life in an institution but it is hard indeed to achieve in the complexity of big cities with their shifting populations.

This is one of the reasons why we are beginning to talk about community development methods as something that may be as important for us as for newly developing countries. The impetus comes from the creation of the new towns and new housing estates with their uprooted populations which take time to cohere, and generate problems of mental health, of delinquency and of withdrawal and loneliness in the process. It also comes from new understanding that people need to feel the warmth of small groups to which they belong and through which they have some control over what happens to them and to their surroundings. This is as true of the cog-in-the-machine feeling of the worker in great enterprises as it is of the mother who does not know anyone who would lend a hand in an emergency. Community development essentially consists in bringing people with common interests together to discuss their most pressing needs and decide what could be done both by them and by public and voluntary services to meet these needs. Councils of social service, settlements and community centres, tenants' association and mutual aid societies are well known forms of community development organizations. But new forms need to be created, perhaps on a wider scale, less attached to a building, more flexible in their methods than the old forms. Community development must also be based on research findings in the fields of social relationships, motivation, small group theory and social action. It must also distil from theory and empirical action its own body of knowledge, to be applied in practice.

The presence of the social workers has been implicit in all that has been said so far. Their presence must now be made explicit, especially from the angle of where to use them and how to equip them for their task. Current thinking, though only to a limited extent current practice, suggests that deployment has not received the attention it deserves. The under fives have been cited as an obvious point at which we should deploy some of our best resources of social workers and others, children at school are another obvious group where early detection of difficulty could lead to family help. This is the philosophy of the fence at the top of the cliff rather than the ambulance at the bottom, though there is no denying the need for the ambulance too.

So far as the equipment of the social worker is concerned, the best available training and opportunities for further professional development in employment has been in casework with a rather limited range of clients. This is changing with growing interest in gaining more systematic understanding of how to 'motivate the unmotivated client'; the delinquent for example who sees nothing wrong with himself and no need for change; of how to communicate with the inarticulate; of how to help the immature and those with a poorly developed sense of social obligation to react more appropriately to other people and to the demands of social living. All this is leading to more flexible approaches than the one-to-one interview. New light on family interaction, on the potency of group action and discussion, on the crucial importance of communication and relationship in human affairs, is leading to much more experiment with multiple interviewing and group work. This may be in small groups, whether of parents whose children are on probation; or would-be adoptive parents; or handicapped people; or ex-mental hospital patients; or alcoholics or others. Or it may consist of clubs, divided into a number of small groups, and with a variety of activities to help people who find difficulty in social relationships – or who just plain enjoy doing things together.

So far, group work is but little developed in this country as a social work method. The impetus is now coming from some of the foregoing developments, from some segments of the youth service and from the expansion of group psychiatry, which has led to a more general interest in group dynamics. Social work is thus faced, as in the early days of casework, with the dual task of taking over knowledge from group dynamics and small group theory and learning how to use this appropriately and to extend it through work with groups.

There are those who say that community development is simply social work with individuals and groups writ large, since the community can only be composed of individuals and groups in interaction with each other. There are also those who hold that this multiple inter-action in itself constitutes a dimension calling for further knowledge and skill. However that may be, almost all's to do in pioneering community development in this country as a consciously guided process and in creating the necessary body of knowledge and skill.

It can hardly be said that the outlook for social work is either humdrum or clear cut. It is indeed a profession in its early beginnings with far more tasks ahead of it than it yet knows how to fulfil.

I. Training for social work

Methods of training for different branches of social work have been frequently mentioned in the preceding pages. In the appendix practical instruction on training for all kinds of social work is brought together. It is not easy for the would-be social worker to make sense of the fairly complicated patterns of training which exist in Britain today. No-one is satisfied with the present situation and attempts are being made to create a more rational system out of the present maze. This is bound to take time in a country which values both its history and its democratic methods of dealing with social change.

Whilst the following outlines of methods of training is comprehensive, it has not been possible to give very much detail or to explain fully the connection between one type of training and another. Many organizations mentioned in this Appendix should be able not only to give fuller information but also to redirect the enquirer if he or she happens to have written for information to the wrong source.

A list of comprehensive sources of additional information is given at the end of the Appendix.

UNIVERSITY COURSES

(a) *Basic courses* (*Not professional training in social work*)

The most common method for students who know from the outset that they wish to work in the social services is to begin by studying for a Degree in Social Studies or in Sociology. Some of these Degree courses include practical work of an introductory nature and are therefore more relevant than others. It is wise to consult before-hand the Joint University Council for Social and Public Administration, or one of the professional organizations (see list at the end of Appendix).

For those who read Degrees in other subjects it is normally necessary to take a post-graduate diploma (usually one year) in Social Studies or Social Science before being admitted to a course of professional train-ing (but see also (b) (iii) below).

As an alternative to reading for a Degree it is possible to study for a Diploma or Certificate in Social Science (generally lasting two years). University entrance qualifications are usually required (but not at every university) and candidates must be older and have had at least a year's employment experience. The minimum age is usually 19 or 20 and sometimes more.

The University of London awards an External Diploma in Social Studies. This Diploma is a recognized qualifi-cation for most professional training courses. Study for the Diploma may be undertaken on a part-time basis or at full-time courses in certain colleges of further education in various parts of the country. Part-time students are required to complete a maximum of six months *full-time* practical work. This course should not be confused with the Extension Diploma in Sociology of the University of London. It is possible, in certain circumstances, however, for holders of this Diploma to gain exemption from the theoretical work for the Ex-ternal Diploma in Social Studies.

Further information about the post-graduate diploma and two-year courses can be obtained from the Joint University Council. Enquiries concerning the External Diploma should be made to the External Registrar, The University of London, Senate House, W.C.1.

(b) P fessional training courses in social work

A student who has successfully completed one of the

courses listed in (*a*) may then apply for training in social work. These courses fall into four main categories, all of which have a planned programme of practical work under the supervision of experienced social workers:

(i) *Applied social studies courses.* A growing number of universities arrange courses of professional training which are generic. This means that students who wish to prepare themselves for a specialist field of work can train alongside others in a course which seeks to emphasize the common element in the knowledge which is applicable to social work and in the methods used by social workers. Students completing these courses are recognized as qualified by the specialist bodies which have approved them. Not every course is able to provide specialist training for all the fields.

(ii) *Specialist courses.* Some universities provide courses of specialist training which lead to recognition by the organizations concerned – for example, psychiatric social work.

(iii) In certain universities there are special courses for graduates who have read less relevant degrees. These courses are recognized for the Child Care and Probation Services only. They combine academic study of the Social Sciences with professional training and replace the need for the separate post-graduate diploma courses in Social Studies.

(iv) *Specialist courses outside the universities for students with university basic qualifications.* There are a number of training courses outside the universities for which a Degree or Diploma from a university is a necessary entry qualification. These include training for Probation (provided by the Home Office), Medical Social Work (provided by the Institute of Medical Social Workers), Moral Welfare (provided by Josephine Butler House, Liverpool). Some voluntary organizations provide an inservice training for family caseworkers.

EXTRA-MURAL AND NON-UNIVERSITY COURSES

The Child Care Service (including appropriate voluntary organizations

The Central Training Council in Child Care (Home Office) arranges two main types of course for people without Degrees or Social Studies Diplomas:

(i) Two-year courses for students over 25. These courses are sometimes in extra-mural departments and sometimes in colleges of further education. Candidates must have sufficient ability and education to follow the courses successfully in addition to having the necessary personal qualities.

(ii) One-year courses. Candidates must have either considerable experience in child care or have some other relevant training and experience, e.g. teachers, health visitors, etc.

The health and welfare services (and voluntary organizations providing similar services)

The Council for Training in Social Work promotes two-year courses in social work. The syllabus for these courses seeks to emphasize the general principles applicable in social work whilst providing some specialist teaching appropriate to the health and welfare and hospital services. The minimum age for these courses is 19 but preference is given to older candidates. The educational entry requirements for those who are under 25 are one 'A' level and three 'O' levels or five 'O' levels (this must include one subject which tests the capacity to use the English language). For those who are over 25 it is necessary for candidates to show that they have the ability to follow the course successfully as well as having the necessary personal qualities. The Council also promotes special courses for those older members of staff who are employed in the health and welfare services or in voluntary organizations with similar functions.

It is also possible for some students who are considering entering the hospital service (but not as medical social workers or psychiatric social workers) to study these courses.

Moral welfare

A three-year course is provided at Josephine Butler House, Liverpool, in conjunction with the Social Science Certificate Course at the University of Liverpool. There is also a two-year non-university course. Candidates should normally be between the ages of 23 and 45. The course is residential and inter-denominational.

The Probation and After Care Service

One-year courses of training for the Probation and After Care Service are arranged by the Home Office in a number of centres. The minimum age for candidates is 27 and they must show ability to follow the course successfully as well as having the necessary personal qualities.

Further information. Details of these courses can be obtained from the Central Training Council in Child Care, the Probation and After Care Council, Council for Training in Social Work and Josephine Butler House (see list below).

OTHER BRANCHES OF SOCIAL WORK AND RELATED SERVICES

The main focus of training in the courses listed above is on case work with individuals and families. There is a growing interest, however, in work with groups and communities. Some of the work with groups may take place in residential institutions.

Group work

Some universities are providing within the context of training for youth work a post-graduate course in Social

Group Work. Another university department of education provides one-year courses in youth leadership for graduates and mature non-graduate students. Training is also provided at the National College for the Training of Youth Leaders, Humberstone Drive, Leicester and Westhill College, Birmingham. The Y.W.C.A. and the National Association of Youth Clubs offer training courses for their own workers. Further information about Group Work may be obtained from:

The Further Education Branch of the Department of Education and Science
Curzon Street, London W.1
(or from Local Education Authorities)

The Standing Conference of Youth Organizations
The National Old People's Welfare Council
26 Bedford Square, London W.C.1

The National Association for Mental Health
39 Queen Anne Street, London W.1

Some Teacher Training Colleges offer a Youth Service option or bias as part of their three-year course.

Community work

There is no specific training for Community Work at present but advice and information may be obtained from:

The National Federation of Community Associations
26 Bedford Square, London W.C.1
The British Association of Residential Settlements
Bishop Creighton House, 378 Lillie Road S.W.6

Work with the blind and the deaf

Training for social work with the blind and the deaf is at present under review. Further information can be obtained from:

The Council for Training in Social Work
Clifton House, Euston Road, London N.W.1

The Southern Regional Association for the Blind
14 Howick Place, Victoria, London, S.W.1

The social workers

The North Regional Association for the Blind
Headingley Castle, Headingley Lane, Leeds 6

The Western Regional Association for the Blind
39 East Street, Newton Abbot, Devon

The Scottish National Federation for the Blind
4 Coates Crescent, Edinburgh

Wales and Monmouthshire Regional Council for the Blind
Llandelyn, Folland Road, Garnant, South Wales

College of Deaf Welfare and Social Studies
321 Green Lanes, Manor House, London N.4

Residential work

Information concerning training courses for residential work with children can be obtained from the Central Training Council in Child Care, Home Office, Horseferry House, Dean Ryle Street, S.W.1.

The National Old People's Welfare Council, 26, Bedford Square, London, W.C.1. will provide information about training courses for Matrons and Wardens for Old People's Homes.

Teaching of the mentally handicapped

For those interested in teaching mentally sub-normal children and adults, information about training courses can be obtained from the Secretary, Training Council for Teachers of the Mentally Handicapped, The Ministry of Health, Alexander Fleming House, Elephant and Castle, S.E.1.

OPPORTUNITIES FOR THE POTENTIAL VOLUNTEER

Restriction of space prevents the inclusion of all names of local voluntary organizations. Those who would like further information might refer to a publication called: *Voluntary social services – A handbook of information and directory of organizations* obtainable from the National Council of Social Service, 26, Bedford Square,

W.C.1. (12/6d). This contains a summary of about 300 societies concerned with every aspect of social welfare.

Greater detail of the actual help needed is to be found in a number of local directories for example, the handbook *Some opportunities for voluntary service in London*, London Council of Social Service, 4, Gower Street, W.C.1. (1/9d).

A Government publication of general interest that describes all areas in which voluntary services operate and lists how to get in touch with them is invaluable. *A guide to voluntary service* by David Hobman, H.M.S.O.

Local information can be obtained from various sources including Citizen's Advice Bureaux, local Councils of Social Service, Post Offices and Town Halls where the local register of charitable trusts is available. Telephone directories will indicate initial points of contact.

Publications

For a detailed and comprehensive list of all training schemes up to date: *Training and employment in social work* obtainable from The National Council of Social Service, 26, Bedford Square, London, W.C.1., or The Women's Employment Federation, 251, Brompton Road, London, S.W.3. (5/-).

Two other useful publications are:

Preparation for careers in social work – published by The Joint University Council for Social and Public Administration, 218 Sussex Gardens, W.2

Social work in the *Choice of careers* series (No. 102) of the Ministry of Labour obtainable from H.M.S.O.

Addresses for further information
University: basic and professional courses

The Joint University Council for Social and Public Administration
218 Sussex Gardens, London W.2

The social workers

National Training Organizations

The Central Training Council in Child Care
Home Office, Horseferry House, Dean Ryle Street, London S.W.1

Church of England Council for Social Work
Church House, Dean's Yard, London S.W.1
(Moral Welfare)

The Council for Training in Social Work
Clifton House, Euston Road, London N.W.1

The Probation and After Care Advisory Council
Home Office, Horseferry House, Dean Ryle Street, London S.W.1

Information about training for Probation and Child Care in Scotland and Northern Ireland can be obtained from the appropriate Government Departments.

FINANCE

Finance for students undertaking university basic courses is normally provided through the Local Education Authorities in England and Wales and the Scottish Education Department. As far as university professional courses are concerned, the Home Office has grants available for Probation and Child Care candidates; otherwise students are normally financed by Local Education Authorities, etc., or seconded by employing authorities. Some grants are available for medical and psychiatric social work students from the Ministry of Health. Bursaries are available from the Family Welfare Association, 296, Vauxhall Bridge Road, London, S.W.1. for students intending to train as Family Case-workers on Applied Social Studies courses. These candidates are required to work subsequently on the Association's staff. Bursaries are also available for training in Moral Welfare and for the Youth Service.

II. Social service journals

The following list of the principal British journals concerned with the social services may be useful for reference.

General

Case Conference	Case Conference Ltd c/o Mrs R.V. Andrews, 5 Sudbury Gardens, Selborne Road, Croydon, Surrey
Municipal Journal	Municipal Journal Ltd 3 Clements Inn, London W.C.2
Municipal Review	Association of Municipal Corporations 36 Old Queen Street, London S.W.1
New Society	New Society, Cromwell House Fulwood Place, London W.C.1
Social Service Quarterly	The National Council of Social Service 26 Bedford Square, London W.C.1
Social Work	Association of Family Case-workers c/o Mrs Sylvia Brooks, 7 Haslemere Road, London N.8
Times Educational Supplement	Times Publishing Co. Ltd Printing House Square, London E.C.4

Family and Community

B.A.R.S. Bulletin	Miss M. Lewis, Secretary British Association of Residential Settlements, Bishop Creighton House 378 Lillie Road, London S.W.6

The social workers

Bulletin of the Association of Children's Officers	Miss J. D. Cooper, B.A., (editor) Children's Officer County Hall Lewes, Sussex
Children	National Children's Home 85 Highbury Park, London N.5
Child Care	National Council of Associated Children's Homes 85 Highbury Park, London N.5
Child Care News	The Association of Child Care Officers 31 Bernhard Baron Settlement Henriques St, London E.1
Child Education	Evans Bros. Ltd Montague House, Russell Square, London W.C.1
Child's Guardian	National Society for the Prevention of Cruelty to Children 1 Riding House Street, London W.1
Education	Councils and Education Press Ltd 10 Queen Anne Street, London W.1

Health and welfare

British Hospital and Social Service Journal	Law and Government Publications Ltd 27–29 Furnival Street, London E.C.4
British Journal of Psychiatric Social Work	The Association of Psychiatric Social Workers 71 Albany Street, Regent's Park, London N.W.1
Medical Officer	Hodgetts Ltd 72–8 Fleet Street, London E.C.4
Medical Social Work	The Institute of Medical Social Workers 42 Bedford Square, London W.C.1

Appendices

Mental Health	The National Association for Mental Health 39 Queen Anne Street, London W.1
The Health Visitor	Health Visitors' Association 36 Eccleston Square, London S.W.1

Medical

British Medical Journal	British Medical Association Tavistock Square, London W.C.1
Family Doctor	Family Doctor House 47–51 Chalton Street, London W.1
Nursing Mirror	Iliffe Technical Publications Ltd Dorset House, Stamford Street, London, S.E.1
Nursing Times	Macmillan and Co. Ltd St Martin's Street, London W.C.
The Lancet	The Lancet Ltd 7 Adam Street, London W.C.2
Approved Schools Gazette	H. Heathcote Tennal School, Harbourne, Birmingham 32

The offender

Justice of the Peace and Local Government Review	Justice of the Peace Ltd Little London, Chichester, Sussex (London: 88 Kingsway, W.C.2)
Probation	The National Association of Probation Officers 6 Endsleigh Street, London W.C.1

III. The work of voluntary organisations

Personal services to the individual at home
Aids to the infirm sick and handicapped
Assistance with almoning and the administration of local trust funds
Clothing, provision of, in recommended cases
Day and night sitter-in services
Diversional occupations for handicapped
Emergency supplies of fuel, furniture and bedding
Escort services (for the sick, infirm, handicapped and for children)
Gardening
Hair washing, shaving, bathing, foot care
Help in the home
Home nursing requisites (loan or provision of)
House decorating and repairs
Housing problems of the elderly or disabled
Laundry
Library (mobile or special facilities)
Meals on Wheels
Nursing Aid Service (under District Nurse, including simpler personal services, blanket bathing, etc.)
Outings and entertainments
Prevention of accidents
Reading
Shopping, collecting prescriptions and pensions
Tape recordings for the housebound (church services, messages from relatives, etc.)
Transport (by cars and specially adapted vehicles)
Travelling companions (to aged or infirm needing to make a journey)
Visiting housebound and others in need of help
Wireless and T.V. sets (provision and/or repairs)

Community services outside the home
After-care and rehabilitation
Boarding out of old people
Chiropody

Clinics, assistance at (Ante-natal, Child Welfare, Immunization, etc.)

Creches for mentally disordered children

Courses for the elderly ('Making the Most of Retirement,' etc.)

Diversional occupations and trolley shops in local authority homes and voluntary homes

Emergency, e.g., floods, fire; general help

Entertainments

Family Service Units

Family Rehabilitation Centres

Handicraft and other classes

Health education

Help in local authority and voluntary homes (particularly at times of staff shortage or illness)

Holidays (groups and individuals)

Hospital Car Service

Job-finding schemes

Lunch clubs

Residential homes and hostels

Short-stay homes (including convalescent beds and to relieve relatives)

Social and recreational clubs

Training and occupational centres, assistance in

Welfare foods, distribution of

Workshops and sheltered employment schemes

General

Advice and information

Education and research

Publicity for available services

Training courses and conferences for voluntary workers

IN HOSPITAL

Personal care of the patient

Auxiliary Nursing

Escort duties outside hospital (land, sea and air)

Reception and escorting of in-patients and out-patients inside hospital

Feeding of individual patients

Additional services in psychiatric units
Personal appearance of patients

Personal needs of the patient
Shops, Trolley Shops and shopping errands
Canteens (out-patients and visitors)
Telephone trolleys
Care of relatives visiting dangerously ill patients, hospitality and general help, including visiting relatives at home
Care of children whose mothers are attending hospital for treatment or whose parents are visiting patients
Visiting and befriending lonely patients
Reading (especially arranging short-term attachment of regular readers to patients undergoing eye operation)
Writing letters
Interpreter services for foreign patients

Additional services in psychiatric units
Befriending or 'Godmother' schemes for lonely patients without family or friends
Escorting patients, e.g., to Church, to the cinema, to the dentist, to shops, for picnics and out to tea

Additional services in geriatric units
Outings
Holidays away from hospitals

Additional services in paediatric and maternity units
Escorting children to and from hospitals and out-patient clinics when it is impossible for mothers to do so
Taking convalescent children for walks
Visiting child long-term patients in hospitals some distance from their homes
Collecting mother's milk for premature babies or those with gastro-enteritis
Issuing Welfare Foods in out-patient clinics

Recreation and occupations
Libraries, including film and picture libraries

Handcrafts: Sewing, knitting, weaving, canework and other suitable bedside crafts

Hobbies: Painting, stamp collecting, jig saw puzzles, cards, chess, games

Television

Entertainments: Music, dramatics, youth organization groups in long-term hospitals

Additional services in psychiatric units

Handcrafts, including workshop facilities

Social clubs and organization of links with clubs outside

Entertainments:

Concerts, gramophone recitals and community singing

Whist Drives

Dancing (folk and ballroom)

Film shows, dramatics, play-reading

Discussion groups

Social evenings

Art exhibitions

Additional services in geriatric units

Social clubs

Additional services in paediatric units

Reading aloud and story-telling

Games

General work for the hospital

Reinforcement of official nursing and other services in emergency, e.g. epidemic, transport disasters, industrial disasters

General help in wards (non-nursing)

Clerical assistance, relief telephonists, messenger service

Maintenance activities (work parties):

Sewing, knitting, mending and sorting linen

Making dressings

General help with ward teas and suppers

Gardens, general help

Flower arranging

Bibliography

The following list of books is a selection of useful background reading on aspects of social work.

Historical background

BRUCE, M. *The coming of the welfare state.* Batsford, 1961. 35s

MARSHALL, T. H. *Social policy.* Hutchinson, 1965. 15s

DONNISON, D. V. *The development of social administration* (L.S.E. Inaugural Lecture). Bell, 1962. o.p.

WOODROFFE, K. *From charity to social work in England and the United States.* Routledge, 1962. 30s

YOUNG, A. F. and ASHTON, E. T. *British social work in the nineteenth century.* Routledge, 1956. 25s

OWEN, D. *English philanthropy, 1660–1960.* Harvard U.P.; O.U.P., 1965. 70s

HALL, M. P. *The social services of modern England.* Routledge, 6th edn., 1963. 28s

General background

YOUNGHUSBAND, E. *Social work and social change.* Allen & Unwin, 1964. 21s

CARNEGIE UNITED KINGDOM TRUST. *Social work in Britain;* by E. Younghusband. Dunfermline: The Trust, 1951

NATIONAL INSTITUTE FOR SOCIAL WORK TRAINING. *Introduction to a social worker.* Allen & Unwin, 1964. 15s; paperback 8s 6d

BRITISH BROADCASTING CORPORATION. *Women and work.* BBC, 1965

MINISTRY OF HEALTH AND DEPARTMENT OF HEALTH FOR SCOTLAND. *Report of the working party on social workers in the local authority health and welfare services* (Younghusband report). H.M.S.O., 1959. 15s

FAMILY SERVICE ASSOCIATION OF AMERICA. *Interviewing – its principles and methods;* by A. Garrett. The Assoc., 1951

M. ROOFF. *Voluntary societies and social policy.* Routledge, 1957.

NATIONAL COUNCIL OF SOCIAL SERVICE. *Communities and social change: implications for social welfare.* N.C.S.S., 1964. 3s

BIESTEK, F. *The casework relationship.* Allen & Unwin, 1961. 18s

TIMMS, N. *Social casework: principles and practice.* Routledge, 1964. 25s

Family welfare

POLITICAL AND ECONOMIC PLANNING. *Family needs and the social services.* P.E.P.; Allen & Unwin, 1961. 30s

HOME OFFICE. *Report of the committee on children and young persons* (Ingleby report). H.M.S.O., 1960. 8s. Cmnd. 1191

KASTELL, J. *Casework in child care.* Routledge, 1962. 35s

STROUD, J. *An introduction to the child care service.* Longmans, 1965. 10s 6d

BOWLBY, J. *Child care and the growth of love,* based on '*Maternal care and mental health*' a report prepared for the World Health Organization; abridged and ed. by M. Fry. Penguin Books, 1953. 4s 6d

BRILL, K. *Children, not cases.* National Children's Home, 1962. 10s 6d

BRILL, K. and THOMAS, R. *Children in homes.* Gollancz, 1964. 25s

FORD, D. *The deprived child and the community.* Constable, 1955. 20s

HEMMING, J. *Problems of adolescent girls.* Heinemann, 1960. 21s

HEYWOOD, J. *Children in care.* Routledge, 1959. 25s

WINNICOTT, D. W. *The child, the family and the outside world.* Penguin Books, 1964. 4s 6d

WINNICOTT, C. *Child care and social work.* Welwyn: Codicote, P. 1964. 8s 6d

PHILP, A. F. *Family failure.* Faber, 1963. 32s 6d

STOTT, D. H. *Unsettled children and their families.* U.L.P., 1956. 18s

WYNN, M. *Fatherless families.* Joseph, 1964. 25s

The disabled and the handicapped

BRITISH COUNCIL FOR REHABILITATION OF THE DISABLED. *The handicapped school leaver.* B.C.R.D., 1964. 15s

MINISTRY OF LABOUR. *Services for the disabled.* H.M.S.O., 2nd edn., 1961. 8s 6d

NATIONAL COUNCIL OF SOCIAL SERVICE. *Help for the handicapped.* N.C.S.S., 1958

The community and youth

KUENSTLER, P. H. K. (ed.). *Social group work in Great Britain.* Faber, 1955. o.p.

NATIONAL COUNCIL OF SOCIAL SERVICE. *Community organisation: an introduction.* N.C.S.S., 1962. 7s 6d

SPENCER, J. *Stress and release in an urban estate.* Tavistock P., 1964. 45s

ROSS, M. G. *Community organisation.* Harper, 1955. $3

BATTEN, T. R. *Training for community development.* O.U.P., 1962. 22s 6d

NATIONAL COUNCIL OF SOCIAL SERVICE. *Working with communities;* ed. R. T. Clarke. N.C.S.S, 1964. 6s 6d

JENNINGS, H. *Societies in the making.* Routledge, 1962. 32s

MORSE, M. *The unattached.* Penguin Books, 1964. 3s 6d

MINISTRY OF EDUCATION. *The youth service in England and Wales* (Albemarle report). H.M.S.O., 1960. 6s. Cmnd. 929

Problems of old age

COLE, D. and UTTING, J. E. G. *The economic circumstances of old people.* Welwyn: Codicote P., 1962. 12s 6d

RICHARDSON, I. M. *Age and need: a study of older people in North-East Scotland.* Livingstone, 1964. 25s

TOWNSEND, P. *The family life of old people* (Institute of Community Studies report no. 2). Routledge, 1957. 30s; Penguin Books, 1963. 5s

Bibliography

TOWNSEND, P. *The last refuge: a survey of residential institutions and homes for the aged in England and Wales.* Routledge, 1962. 60s

NATIONAL OLD PEOPLE'S WELFARE COUNCIL. *Age is opportunity.* N.C.S.S., 2nd edn. 1961. 8s 6d

HILL, M. N. *An approach to old age and its problems.* Oliver & Boyd, 1961. 15s

SLACK, K. *Councils, committees and concern for the old.* Welwyn: Codicote, P., 1960. 7s 6d

NATIONAL OLD PEOPLE'S WELFARE COUNCIL. *Planning for ageing: report of the 12th National Conference on the care of the elderly.* N.C.S.S., 1964. 5s

Medical social work

BELL, E. M. *The birth of a profession.* Faber, 1961. o.p.

COLLINS, J. *Social casework in a general medical practice.* Pitman Medical, 1965. 30s

Mental health

MILLS, E. *Living with mental illness: a study in East London* (Institute of Community Studies report no. 7). Routledge, 1962. 28s

ADAMS, M. ed. *The mentally subnormal: the social casework approach.* Heinemann, 1960. 25s

TIZARD, J. *Community services for the mentally handicapped.* O.U.P., 1964. 28s

The offender

WALKER, N. *Crime and punishment in Britain.* Edinburgh U.P., 1965. 70s

SINGTON, D. and PLAYFAIR, G. *Crime, punishment and cure.* Secker & Warburg, 1965. 45s

NATIONAL ASSOCIATION OF PROBATION OFFICERS. *The probation service;* ed. J. F. S. King. Butterworth, 2nd edn., 1964. 30s

MONGER, M. *Casework in probation.* Butterworth, 1964. 35s

HOWARD, D. L. *The English prisons.* Methuen, 1960. 21s

KLARE, H. J. *Anatomy of prison.* Hutchinson, 1960. 18s

MORRIS, P. *Prisoners and their families.* Allen & Unwin, 1965. 50s; 21s paperback

MORRIS, T. and MORRIS, P. *Pentonville*. Routledge, 1963. 50s

TURNER, M. *A pretty sort of prison.* Pall Mall P., 1964. 25s

HOME OFFICE. *Report of interdepartmental committee on the business of the criminal courts* (Streatfeild report). H.M.S.O., 1960. 8s 6d. Cmnd. 1289

HOME OFFICE. *Report of the advisory council on the treatment of offenders, sub-committee on the organisation of after-care.* H.M.S.O., 1963. 5s 6d

HOME OFFICE. *Penal practice in a changing society.* H.M.S.O., 1959. 3s. Cmnd. 645

The voluntary contribution

TREASURY, *A guide to voluntary service*; by D. Hobman. H.M.S.O., 1964. 3s 6d

BEVERIDGE, Lord. *Voluntary action: a report on methods of social advance.* Allen & Unwin, 1948. o.p.

NATIONAL COUNCIL OF SOCIAL SERVICE. *The role of the voluntary services in contemporary Britain*; by Sir H. Hetherington. N.C.S.S., 1963. 2s

NATIONAL COUNCIL OF SOCIAL SERVICE. *Social enterprise: a study of the activities of voluntary organisations in an industrial town;* by M. Morris. N.C.S.S., 1962. 7s 6d